The
HOUSE
in
ANTIGUA

A Restoration

By

LOUIS ADAMIC

ILLUSTRATED

Harper & Brothers *Publishers*

NEW YORK *and* LONDON

1937

To
the Memory of
DOROTHY HUGHES POPENOE

*

Contents

ILLUSTRATIONS

*

*The illustrations, grouped as a separate
section, will be found following page 150*

[ix]

Illustrations

[x]

To begin with—
THE TRIP

*"And, oh, don't fail to
see the Popenoe place!"*

Early in December of 1936 some friends
of mine returned from a brief trip to Guatemala
enthusiastic almost to the point of inarticulateness
(not their usual state) about that Central American
country. They seemed particularly excited
about its former capital, once known as Santiago
de los Caballeros de Guatemala, now called Antigua
(Old Town), which was a vital and important
city when Boston, New York, Philadelphia,

[3]

and Charleston were not yet embryos in the womb
of Time; and which was destroyed by earthquake
in 1773 and then abandoned as capital, to remain
for the most part a ruin to this day.

Without knowing just why, I had long been responsive to these lines in the second act of *The
Mikado*:

> *There's a fascination frantic*
> *In a ruin that's romantic—*

Some years ago—on the way to Yugoslavia—I
had stopped at Naples and spent six of the fullest
hours of my life wandering about in Pompeii with
a loquacious, well-informed guide. Then, in Yugoslavia, I had gone several times to Solin, the ruined
Roman town not far from Split, in central Dalmatia, which was in the process of being excavated
just then; and had also visited a number of
archæological diggings in Macedonia.

So now I suddenly booked passage for the land
of the quetzal-bird, intending to put up in the
ruined old city for two or three weeks. New York's
frenzied confusions and vivid complexities had

lately been becoming a strain; I wanted "to get away from it all for a while," and Antigua appeared ideal for my purpose. I was told that it was not only quiet and restful, but "practically dead," at the same time that, strange as it might seem, it was living fully up to Aldous Huxley's recent description of it as "one of the most romantic cities in the world."

The hotel there, I understood, was not bad, nor expensive. It received only an occasional overnight guest. Once a fortnight or so a crowd of tourists, in charge of guides, passed through the town in motor-cars, causing a little disturbance, but as a rule they remained only a couple of hours around lunch time. Whereupon the hush of the centuries again settled on the city.

"And, oh, when in Antigua," exclaimed my just-returned friends, "don't fail to see the Popenoe place!" and, their faces glowing, they tried to tell me about the lovely, painstakingly restored three-hundred-year-old house that had been a ruin for a hundred and sixty years.

Waiting for my sailing date to come around, I

The House in Antigua

met others who had been to Guatemala in recent years, and most of them urged me to exert all effort to get inside the Popenoe house in Antigua. It seemed that everybody could not gain entrance. The owner, Doctor Wilson Popenoe, was seldom there, and his housekeeper, a part-Indian woman named Maria, admitted no one without an identifying card from him.

None of these people who were so eager for me to visit his house in Antigua knew Doctor Popenoe, but one or two had met persons who were more or less acquainted with him and his work. Also, impelled by curiosity, I found several lines about him in *Who's Who*. And I learned that he was an internationally known American botanist, pomologist, and soil expert; a one-time agricultural explorer for the Division of Foreign Seed and Plant Introduction of the United States Department of Agriculture; the author of a standard book on tropical and subtropical fruits; for many years now head agronomist ("traveling farmer") of the United Fruit Company, overseeing production on more than one hundred thousand acres of

banana plantations in seven or eight Middle
American countries and directing the fight against
the various diseases attacking the banana plant;
and the creator of a tropical experimental garden
in the jungles of Lancetilla Valley, near the port
of Tela, in Honduras, which was his headquarters.

He was called "Doctor" in Latin America by
virtue of an honorary degree which the University
of San Marcos at Lima, Peru, the oldest institution
of higher learning in the New World, had conferred upon him in 1924 in recognition of his con-
tributions to the knowledge of plant life in the
American tropics. Also, in Central and South
America scientific men are generally "Doctors,"
whether they have a degree or not.

To intimates, Wilson Popenoe was simply
"Pop."

I learned, too, that the lately restored house in
Antigua, which so excited nearly every one who
had seen it, was less his achievement than his
wife's; and that she—Dorothy Hughes Popenoe,
also a botanist and an archæologist of note, but
dead since 1932—had been a most extraordinary
young woman.

[7]

I meet Wilson Popenoe

A CAREFULLY RESTORED DWELLING IN A ruined or partly ruined city. . . .

Something fine and finished in the midst of wreckage. ——

Listening to my friends, I caught some of their enthusiasm about the house. I was shown a snapshot of a portion of it. It began to interest me as a situation and an idea. And presently my motive for going to Guatemala was not only "to get away from it all," but to see the Popenoe house.

[8]

The Trip

How to meet this man Popenoe, or at least secure a card from him that would get me past
Maria when I reached Antigua? I imagined her
to be a most formidable person.

My ship, a banana-boat, was stopping in Tela;
and, inquiring at the United Fruit office in New
York while getting my ticket if I might not see
Popenoe while in port there, I was informed that,
continually on the go in the wet coastal tropics
when not upon hurried trips to the United States
for conferences at the Company's general offices
in Boston, he was at Tela well-nigh as infrequently
as in Antigua. They could not tell me where he
was just then. Perhaps on some plane, train, ship,
cayuco, or mule's back, going or returning some
place. One or two had never seen him; they knew
him only by name and reputation. Others had just
glimpsed him as he rushed off, or to, his ship. He
was one of the most traveled men in the world.

A week before sailing, however, I chanced to
see Samuel Zemurray, the big boss of the United
Fruit, whom I had met a few times before; and
who, on being told that I was going to Guatemala,

talked to me for an hour or longer about the Indians of Middle America and their ways, then remarked that I ought to meet "Pop," who would be
in New York the following morning at ten, Hon-
duras-bound from Boston, catching a boat at
eleven. Could I not go down to the dock about
that time and ——?

In the morning I did go to the dock and, a few
minutes before sailing-time, succeeded in seeking
out Wilson Popenoe. He was a tall, sparely-fash-
ioned, graying man in his mid-forties, with a
boyish face etched by suffering. His pleasant manner was compounded of instinctive eagerness,
nervous energy, and almost morbid modesty.

We talked, getting acquainted . . . and he
said he would make his brief semiannual visit to
Antigua about Christmas time, when I was due
there: would I not, upon arrival, come directly to
the house and stay with him?

I thought I had not understood him correctly,
so he repeated the invitation, adding that it was a
big house and there was lots and lots of room. He
himself would be there, alas! only a week or ten

days. But I could stay on if I wished, make myself at home. Maria, who he thought was not the world's worst cook, would take care of me. If nothing else, she would feed me tortillas, tamales, black-bean soup and paste, enchiladas, avocados, pineapple, platanos, and other such native fare, which was so abundant and inexpensive in and around Antigua that Gargantua himself would have been hard put to consume thirty cents' worth of it a day.

We stood in the mid-December cold of the ship's deck and laughed. Antigua seemed more and more attractive.

Doctor Popenoe gave me a card to present to Maria in case I reached the old town before he did, explaining regretfully that this was necessary. Formerly, when he had allowed her to admit any-one who desired to go through the place, people had scribbled their names on the walls, appropri-ated things from the rooms as souvenirs, felt free to pull books from the shelves, peered into closed drawers, broken twigs from the trees, and pulled up plants and flowers in the patios.

The House in Antigua

The gong for "All visitors ashore!" sounded and the gangplank was being unfastened.

"Well," smiled Wilson Popenoe, "see you in Antigua."

"So long!" I said.

"So long! Adiós!"

Going down the gangplank, I became very conscious—without realizing just why—that I had met a man whom I wanted to know better, no less than I wanted to see his house in Guatemala.

I rap the brass knocker—and wait

ON A BRIGHT, SPRING-WARM FORENOON TWO
weeks later: just after Christmas—following a six-
day ocean voyage; an eleven-hour train ride from
the dank, hot sea-level of Puerto Barrios to the
dry, bracing five-thousand-feet altitude of Guatemala City; a two-hour bus trip through the awesome barrancas, or ravines, between the new
capital and Antigua; and a glimpse of some of
the largest, most obvious ruins in the old town—
I rapped the heavy brass knocker shaped like a

[13]

lion on the large and heavy wooden door of a white one-storey house whose exterior, apart from the door, with its many bronze studs, and the handsomely turned wooden grilles over the four high windows in front, was not especially exciting, nor otherwise impressive, on first sight.

Waiting for a response to my knock, I looked down the quiet, cobbled street of very simple one-storey houses, most of which, as I saw later, were still partly wrecked inside.

Three blocks away was the great ruin of the San Francisco church and monastery, and seemingly just beyond and above it, but really miles distant, loomed the volcano Agua, extinct perhaps these last ten or twenty thousand years, its peaceful crater more than twelve thousand feet above the sea. The huge mountain, shaped like the crown of a much-worn Central American sombrero, was brown-green against the clear blue sky, with a neat cloud-ring like an immense white wreath round it half a mile or so below the summit.

A young woman came around the nearest

corner and, heading toward me, drew my gaze and mind from Agua. She was small and dark, perhaps mostly Indian, in her twenties, and not strikingly handsome facially, but on her head she carried a beautifully shaped earthenware water-jug and walked erect and dignified beneath it. Large, almost spherical, with handles near the mouth, the jug rested on a flat, circular pad on her skull without the help of her hands.

She was barefooted, with long, dusty, upturned toes, and clad in a patched skirt and frayed, torn blouse, neither very clean and both partly covered by a vividly striped shawl, one end of it thrown over the shoulder. She passed me proudly, with a simple sufficiency and an all-around economy of being about her. Her blood was mixed, but she was something definite, satisfying to eye and mind.

She somehow reminded me at once of the Nike of Samothrace and a Tanagra figurine, and I could not help but turn around to watch her till she entered a house a few doors north of where I stood.

Her walk was not a poorly arranged collection of movements and jerks of her feet, legs, torso, shoulders, arms, hands, neck and head, which is the general manner of walking in most of the world; rather, from toes to scalp, her body was a rhythmic roll of muscles, flexing and unflexing rapidly in cohesive sequence, which gave the illusion of gliding. She went directly and smoothly forward without side-sways. So supple and pliant, she seemed jointless.

Since reaching the Guatemalan highlands, I had glimpsed, or gazed upon, many of these women bearing rotund water-jugs, baskets, bales, or bundles on their heads, and many of them, too, babies strapped on their backs. Each had seemed a study in form, color, and movement. Each had caused me to recall Samuel Zemurray's words to me in New York two weeks before, which he had repeated two or three times: "They've got something, those people down there; they've got something," meaning especially the Indians and those with a goodly intermixture of Indian blood in their veins.

During the bus ride that I had just completed, from Guatemala City to Antigua, I had seen par-

ticularly graceful girls and women. Near the village of Mixco, for instance, there had been whole
crowds of them bound for the market-place, jog-
ging along the wayside in single file or in pairs,
barefooted, beneath enormous baskets. They half
ran, swinging their arms loosely, flail-like; the
while their small, straight, deep-bosomed torsos
were motionless, save for the rhythm that flowed
into them from the movements of the rest of their
bodies.

Here and there I had caught sight of a face
that was nothing short of lovely, but even the ugly
and plain women had charm. Only their charm
was not a matter of cosmetics, training or conscious
acquisition, but an inherent quality, natural,
racial, not individually personal.

They were like ripples in a river. . . .

Coming up from Puerto Barrios, the train had
stopped for a few minutes at a station along the
Motagua River, perhaps not quite two-thirds of
the way to Guatemala City, near the two-thou-
sand-foot elevation; and, as was usual at these

small depots, there had been about a score of
women and young girls with baskets and bowls of
hard-boiled eggs, fried chicken, and tortillas;
oranges, granadas, bananas, chicos, tomatoes, and
other vegetables and fruits, some of which I had
never seen before. I had leaned out of the car
window, and one of these women, neither very
young nor old, offered me the fruits in her basket.
There was something subtly appealing about her,
and I bought some oranges, although I already
had a hatful inside the car. Whereupon, indifferent whether or not she sold any more that day,
she stayed under my window and, looking up,
talked to me.

She just talked—somewhat in the style in which
Gertrude Stein writes; only naturally, spontane-
ously, without striving for effect of any sort.

My Spanish was scanty. However, less from her
words than from her gestures, her facial expression, the intonation of her speech, and her whole
manner, which was at once open and subdued, I
gathered that she was interested in whether I was
enjoying my trip. Did I like the river? She pointed

at it with unmistakable pride. Was it not a fine river, this Rio Motagua, that ran into the great ocean down below where I came from?

I agreed, and—very much like a child, repeating words and phrases as in a roundelay, and her face as though dazzled by an excessive light which came both from the sun and from something within her—she affirmed that everybody liked Rio Motagua, which was a great noble river. How could they help liking it? As a great, noble river, it was something wonderful; anybody could see that. It flowed on and on, ceaselessly it flowed, and no one really knew where all the water came from. There was rain, of course, but only during the wet season; yet the river went on, day and night, never ceasing its run. During the rainy months the river, this magnificent Rio Motagua which everybody liked so well, was bigger and quite muddy, oh, very muddy; not clear and green like this; no, not at all.

A wonderful river . . . oh, magnifico. . . .

She smiled and pointed at the river again, and her gesture was one of suave grace which contained also something troubling and mysterious. Through her flowed a force of human experience as old as Motagua.

Did I not think, she asked, pointing, that the sun's sheen upon the ripples and swirls was nice? I did think so, and she was glad I liked it. Of course she had known that I did, she said; and she was happy the river helped to make my journey pleasant. . . .

The locomotive whistled, the train started, and, with a little wave of her hand and the slightest possible smile, but which held and gave great warmth, she said, "Adiós, señor, adiós!"

Somehow, I enjoyed thinking of her as I stood in front of this house in Antigua, where I was to live during the next two weeks.

*I stumble into a new Chapter of a
long story*

By AND BY THE VENTANILLO, A GRILLED APER-
ture in the door, opened cautiously inward, and
through the tiny iron bars I perceived a large,
loose dark face contemplating me expressionlessly.

The face emitted a vague grunt: or so it
sounded to me. Besides being full of the grinding
of gears during the toboggan-like bus ride, my
ears were popping from the altitude, and I could
not hear well. I interpreted the grunt to be an

inquiry as to what I wished; but then, on a sudden, I forgot what little Spanish I knew, including the usual greeting for the time of the day.

I remembered Wilson Popenoe's card, which I held in my hand, and—recalling (with a mingling of amusement and annoyance at myself) the old speakeasy days in New York—proffered it through one of the little interstices of the ventanillo, and a dark, stumpy hand, which apparently belonged to the same person as the face, reached for it.

Followed a long moment during which the dark visage within disappeared from my view . . . whereupon it abruptly turned up again, now illumined with a broad, eager smile of hospitality. There was an elaborate Spanish declamation of welcome. A small door within the large door swung open with a thin, quick squeak in the hinges. And Maria—a short, shapeless, barefooted woman past middle age, sans most of her teeth, and with two black braids hanging down her back and tied together at the ends—greeted me in a flavorsome voice, "Buenos dias, señor! Buenos dias!" as though she had been waiting for me

[22]

with mounting impatience half her life. "Pase adelante, señor, pase adelante!. (Come in!) "

Releasing a flood of Spanish, which, by exercising my imagination, I gathered to mean that the Señor Doctor was somewhere about and would appear presently, Maria led me through the cool, long and high zaguan, or entrance passage, which terminated in a lofty Moorish arch of gray stone.

By the time we got under the arch my eyes were suddenly so filled with the scene I was walking into that I failed to see a slightly protruding stone in the floor of the entranceway and stumbled over it.

At this, Maria burst into speech again, apologizing for the stone and expressing concern. But I barely heard her. . . .

Before me was a spacious patio, some seventy feet square, partly in shade and partly flooded by the bright and mild forenoon sun of the Guatemalan highlands. Half of it was in well-mown lawn; the other half, a luxuriant medley of orange, lime, peach, avocado, coffee, mirto, izote, and

[23]

chirimoya trees and bushes, their leaves of various shapes, sizes, and shades of green: all either fruiting or blooming.

Behind the trees was a large, loose mock-orange shrub, which I did not see till later; its profuse little white flowers emanating a narcissian fragrance that a faint breeze just then wafted toward me.

Most of the tree trunks were girdled by small and great colonies of wild orchids, some on the verge of blossoming, all spreading their devious white roots epiphytically limb-ward.

In the center of this great inner court, and dominating it, stood an immense Capuchin cypress, cone-shaped and candle-straight, twice the height of the house and—I learned this subsequently—about ninety years old. Its dense, broad shadow fell upon a corridor.

Directly opposite the zaguan, against the western wall, was a decorated stone fountain, tazza-like and evidently carved long ago under direct Italian Renaissance influence. The flow from its gently-curved lead waterspouts filled the entire place

with steady, susurrant sounds. And on either side
of the fountain sprawled pinanona plants, their
huge, perforated leaves imbibing the vapors from
the great circular basin.

It was all very informal, almost haphazard-
seeming, but not formless; and, after the plain,
unpromising exterior of the house, exceedingly
dramatic—or was romantic the word?

Along the high-pillared open corridors on two
sides of the patio grew rows of geraniums and
white, red, and yellow roses, interspersed with
clumps of long-stemmed cola ferns; while along
the colonnade walls were distributed heavy old
chests and coffers with wrought-iron bands and
brass studs; solid mahogany and cedar benches
and large, bulging terra-cotta jugs; ancient Mayan
idols, incense vessels, and home implements, all
of stone, unearthed who knows where, when, how,
or by whom; and wide and high open doorways
and grilled medallion windows with wooden shutters, slightly ajar, offering narrow glimpses of the
cool, dim interiors.

In the shade of the largest Mayan idol, near

The House in Antigua

where Maria had left me to wait for my host, a little kitten dozed, purring, its face about to come into the spreading sunlight. . . .

Wilson Popenoe appeared from somewhere, greeting and welcoming me in a way that I again sensed the man's unusual quality (which took me awhile to define). Then, amused by my evident excitement about the place, he led me on a tour of the house and its several patios . . . and I found myself near the beginning of a new chapter of a story that had started to roll through the waves of Time and over the geography of Middle America four centuries ago and, rolling, reached a succession of climaxes and gathered unto itself elements of the epic.

Part One
THE CENTURIES

The story begins beneath Agua

Acting in behalf of God Almighty and His Most Catholic Majesty Charles the Fifth, Hernando Cortés—that ruthless, stout-souled mystic and genius among imperialist-adventurers—conquered Mexico. His central object in the Conquest was to stamp out idolatry. At any rate, that was what he said it was in a letter to the rulers of Spain in 1519:

. . . And always on the day before they (the Indians) are to begin some important enterprise they burn in-

[29]

cense in the temples, and sometimes even sacrifice their own persons, some cutting out their tongues, others their ears, still others slicing their bodies with knives in order to offer to their idols the blood which flows from their wounds; sometimes sprinkling the whole of their temple with blood and throwing it up in the air, and many other fashions of sacrifice they use, so that no important task is undertaken without previous sacrifice having been made. One very horrible and abominable custom they have which should certainly be punished . . . , and that is that whenever they wish to beg anything of their idols, in order that their petition might find more acceptance, they take large numbers of boys and girls and even grown men and women and tear out their hearts and bowels while still alive, burning them in the presence of these idols, and offering the smoke of such burning as a pleasant sacrifice. Some of us have actually seen this done and they say it is the most horrible and frightful thing that they have ever seen. Yet the Indians perform this ceremony so frequently that . . . there can be no year (so far as we have been able up to the present to ascertain) in which they have not sacrificed in this manner [in all their numerous temples] some three or four thousand souls. Your Majesties may therefore perceive whether it is not their duty to prevent such loss and evil, and certainly it will be pleasing to God if by means of and under the protection of your royal Majesties these people are introduced into and instructed in the holy Catholic Faith, and the devotion, trust and hope which they now have in their idols turned so as to repose in the divine power of the true God; for it is certain that if they should serve God with the same faith, fervor and diligence they would work many miracles. And we believe that not without cause has God been pleased to allow this land to be discovered in the name of your royal Majesties, that your Majesties may reap great merit and reward from Him in sending the Gospel to these barbarian people who thus by your Majesties' hands will be received into the true faith; for from what we know of them we believe that by the aid of interpreters who should plainly declare to them the truths of the Holy Faith and the error in which they are, many, perhaps all of them, would very quickly depart from their evil ways and would come to true knowledge. . . .

Cortés then sent his handsome and pious young lieutenant, Don Pedro de Alvarado, to subdue the Indian kingdoms to the south and to bring those territories—now the republics of Guatemala, Honduras, El Salvador, Costa Rica, and Nicaragua—under the Spanish rule.

Alvarado virtually accomplished this with a few hundred of his fellow conquistadores, aided by Indians who came with him from Mexico, in less than five months, between December 1523 and April '24; and he wrote to Cortés reports of his "victories." Encountering rather more resistance than had Cortés in Mexico, he butchered the ruling, religious, and artistic aristocracy of the Indian states, thus destroying the ancient indigenous culture and civilization. He exterminated many entire tribes. And he—close kin to Mussolini's "crusaders of civilization" in Ethiopia four hundred years later—initiated measures whereby the leaderless survivors were subtly enslaved, later to be exploited to the utmost for the benefit of Spanish officials and adventurers.

The conquistadores established the center of their authority for that part of Spain's New World at the base of the long-extinct volcano Agua, in the proximity of some Indian settlements. The location was also near the ever-fuming Fuego, in the tiny, lovely valley of Almolonga, the Place of Gushing Waters—so named long before by the Indians for the many vivid springs and streams that made the region lush and fertile while the five-thousand-foot altitude, the perennially warm sun, and the gentle breezes with the tang of salt water reaching fumblingly from the Pacific through the gap between the two volcanos, collaborated in giving the region what is, perhaps, the most equable and exquisite climate on earth: cool-warm, clear, and bracing—at least during the seven-month rainless season from November until June.

The Spaniards of that day (even such Attilas as Pedro de Alvarado) possessed an innate sense of beauty and an almost unfailing genius for picking lovely townsites.

This new settlement, at first consisting mainly of grass-thatched mud-and-cane huts, was named Santiago de los Caballeros de Guatemala, and Alvarado, having been made governor, adelantado, and captain-general of all the lands south of Mexico and north of Panama, created there his home and headquarters.

Soon a few score of Dominican friars came from the island of Hispaniola, and a bishop and other clergy from Spain. These were followed by a contingent of master artisans . . . and, simultaneously with other buildings, a cathedral was erected at Santiago de los Caballeros; while churches, closely resembling the village edifices in Spain, were built in such important Indian centers as Atitlan, Sololá, Chichicastenango, Chiché, and Quezaltenango: usually on the foundations of demolished native temples.

Livestock, seeds, and farm implements arrived from the old country. The Indians—having been drawn, more or less, into the Christian religion —were trained and forced to perform the most arduous menial tasks. Fields, groves, and meadows made Agua's lower slopes into a bright patch-quilt of fertility. And by 1540—following a fire in 1536, which had destroyed all its wooden buildings, that were promptly replaced by stone ones—the little city had a well-nigh solid appearance, a pattern of life that passed for what was generally regarded as civilization, and, it seemed, a future.

Meanwhile, Alvarado voyaged to Mexico, to Peru, to Spain, boasting to the world what a mighty conqueror he was, and—possessed by a fanatical drive to enhance the glory of God, the power of the King-Emperor and, far from least, his own prestige and possessions—he roved over

his domain, ruthlessly stamping out what scattered rebellion and idolatry remained among the
aborigines . . . till in 1541, when he was still a
young man and bursting with plans for new im-
perialist adventures, a horse, stumbling upon a
steep ridge, rolled over him and injured him
fatally.

Don Pedro de Alvarado had been dead for
three months, and his widow, Doña Beatriz, had
been acting governor for two, when, on a rainy,
thunderous night toward the end of that year's
unusually bad wet season, a terrific earth-temblor
laid low, in the briefest time, the whole of Santiago de los Caballeros de Guatemala, killing no
insignificant part of its population, which included about five hundred Spaniards and perhaps
as many Indians.

This, however, was but the initial of two in-
stallments of the calamity that befell the colony
that night.

Simultaneously with the destructive earthquake
at Agua's base, a great crash occurred on or near

its summit, seven thousand feet above. There was a long, sharp roar which, not unlike thunder, rolled swiftly and ominously nearer. Then a furious intermixture of water, loose earth, stones, and uprooted trees and bushes descended upon the already ruined town in a swirling, cataclysmic torrent from the mountainside, sweeping the wreckage, animals, and people, dead and alive, before it, over the floor of the valley and beyond, into the chasmic barrancas.

Everyone believed the end of the world imminent.

The great torrent ran for an hour or two. It gradually subsided into a stream and by daybreak ceased altogether.

Doña Beatriz was among the victims of this second phase of the disaster.

For a time the theory was that the three-hundred-feet-deep, bowl-like crater of the long-slumbering Agua had been filled to the rim by the daily downpours of the preceding few months, and that the quake had cracked the side of the vast bowl directly above the Almolonga valley, whereupon the temporary lake had burst out and hurtled down the precipitous slope on the terror-stricken community, drowning or otherwise depriving of life many who had survived the earthquake. There is a fissure in Agua's crater-wall which might support this theory, were it not on a side of the volcano whence the torrent could not easily have descended upon the town with such destructive force, if at all.

Other explanations of this second part of the catastrophe have been advanced from time to time. The most reasonable of these is that a great cloudburst, such as has never occurred since, fell on Agua's slope near the crest and directly above the town coincidentally with the earthquake, its impact crushing the wall of some arroyo not far below the crater; after which the water, sufficient to fill a small lake, bounded down the steep loose ridge, gathering earth, ashes, sand, small stones, boulders, trees, and endless rubble on the way.

At all events, whatever the violent flood's origin, this two-in-one disaster was one of the most complete instances of destruction since Pompeii. Save for a few church and monastery walls and foundations, nothing remains to-day of Guatemala's first capital.

Near the scene there is now a tiny community called Ciudad Vieja, dominated by a squat, unattractive church, built long after the catastrophe in its commemoration.

The following morning, with zopilotes, a species of huge black carrion birds, converging upon the Almolonga valley under the low-hanging sky, the surviving residents of the destroyed capital, shivering with chill and horror, gathered on a ruin and formed a provisional government. The world had not ended and would, to all seeming, continue.

What now? Rebuild the city on the same spot? Move? Where to?

The colonists' ignorance of earthquakes was abysmal. They decided to create a new capital in the Panchoy Valley, which was larger and even lovelier than the Place of the Gushing Waters, only three miles away from Agua's base, and but slightly farther from Fuego than had been the old town; and to call it again Santiago de los Caballeros de Guatemala.

This was the inception of the city now known as Antigua.

Don Luis de las Infantas comes over from old Spain

THE RAINY SEASON ENDED. AID CAME FROM Mexico, from the West Indies, from Spain; but mainly in the form of building craftsmen: masons, stonecutters, carpenters, smiths. The sense of horror gradually passed from the colonists' daily conscious life. The yoke of virtual serfdom was tightened around the necks of tens of thousands of Christianized Indians. Work started. It was pressed. . . . And during the last half of the

[40]

sixteenth century the new city—officially founded in 1543 with a solemn procession to Almolonga and back—rapidly grew into a sizable community. At that time it was inferior in New World importance only to the capitals of Mexico and Peru.

Within half a century a dozen great church edifices and monasteries and many public buildings, with walls three and four feet thick, were erected in the midst of hundreds of new homes, which were all exceedingly modest and simple on the outside, but not a few strikingly attractive within.

Spain was then at the apex of her power. The perceptible beginning of her decline was still a full half-century in the future. Her wealth was immense. It poured in from her colonies. She was, almost literally, Golden Spain.

She could afford daring. She had been enjoying a long period of peace. She had vigor, initiative, some originality, much pride. Her language surpassed other European tongues in strength, pungency, nobility, and delicacy. She had humor and a sense of the dramatic. Romance throbbed in her blood. Her men loved danger. Religious fanaticism, cruelty, and passion for adventure blazed in her eyes. Unconsciously, she worshiped Beauty. She was beginning to produce a spontaneous, earthy literature, which was not great (except for *Don Quixote*) but intensely alive.

She had taken the Renaissance, then spreading through Europe, and married it to the style of architecture she inherited from her old masters, the Moors, with its unimpressive exteriors, lovely inner courts and gardens, and exuberantly rich, half-Oriental, half-African interior decorations; whereupon all manner of interesting and wonderful features commenced to appear in her new churches, civic and military structures, and private dwellings.

Especially in her private dwellings.

The early Renaissance in Spain took the suggestion from the Moors and put the face, the heart, the color, the soul of the house inside. The home became a place of seclusion, a fastness of privacy. With some people, it was also a mark of their outward calm, a symbol of austerity, a state-

ment of their disinclination to crass exhibitionism, a quiet manifestation of their *inner* qualities
—taste, culture, self-control.

And the Spanish colonists brought this Moorish-Renaissance idea with them to America and
made it the principal feature of their Colonial
architecture. In parts of Spain's New World it
prevailed, in the main, for well over a century, a
good spell after it had commenced to degenerate
into flamboyancy and go gingerbread in the homeland.

In the new Santiago de los Caballeros de Guatemala the idea attained its apogee in the second
quarter of the seventeenth century, when the city's
population was about fifty thousand, which number included some ten thousand Indians . . .
when there was a good deal of construction . . .
and when one Doctor don Luis de las Infantas
Mendoza y Venegas arrived from Spain and decided to build the house now the property of
Wilson Popenoe.

Popenoe has had researchers delve into the
archives of both old Spain and Spanish America

for facts concerning this man—with none too abundant results, but which are sufficient to aid imagination in tracing a rough, here and there slightly dim, outline of his life so far as it pertains to the house.

Don Luis de las Infantas Mendoza y Venegas was born in 1595, or slightly over a century after Columbus innocently ran into the New World. His home city was Cordova, whose architecture had long been under strong Moorish and Renaissance influences. He was a son of Don Antonio de las Infantas y Mendoza, also a native of that town; and a grandson of Don Francisco de las Infantas, who had served "in very honorable posts" in the wars against the Moors at Granada.

Don Luis studied law at the universities of Salamanca and Seville, receiving degrees at both institutions.

In 1630, the King named him—according to an old Spanish custom, chiefly in recognition of his grandfather's service in the Moorish wars!—an Oidor de la Real Audiencia de Guatemala, the equivalent of a supreme court justice.

The Centuries

In obedience, perhaps to another venerable Spanish custom, young Don Luis—he was then in his mid-thirties—did not leave for his post for nearly two years after receiving the appointment.

Meanwhile, he married Doña Feliciana de Hermosilla y Armenta, the eighteen-year-old daughter of General Juan de Hermosilla, son of a veteran of the Moorish campaigns who resided in Seville on a thoroughfare—the Calle de Bayona —then remarkable for its Moorish-Renaissance houses, done in the best tradition of that style.

Of Doña Feliciana's life, looks, and character, either prior to or after her union with Don Luis, no definite details are available. But it cannot be doubted that culturally and socially her background was similar to her husband's. They were of the same class.

In all likelihood, she was raised according to the standards of that day, convent-educated, "accomplished," and pretty, or even beautiful. If not, she was indeed an exceptional upper-class Sevillana. Her dowry was undoubtedly considerable. Don Luis had probably been a frequent visitor in their home on the Calle de Bayona while he was a student at Seville.

When finally they embarked for the New World, the Infantas couple took with them six household servants, male and female, among them a twenty-year-old Indian girl from Peru, named Agueda, whom a former Viceroy in Lima, the Marques de Guadalcazar, had brought to Spain some years previous.

The new judge assumed his duties in the Audiencia at Santiago de los Caballeros in the middle of 1632. The ensuing year, for some unknown reason, the Order of Calatrava was conferred upon him—possibly also for being his grandfather's grandson.

Then, early in 1634, when the retiring governor of the colony, Don Diego de Acuña, left the country, Infantas accompanied him on the six-day journey to the seaport and then returned to the capital with the new governor, Don Alvaro de Quiñones Osorio. He had, to all seeming, quickly become a figure of consequence in the New World.

The Centuries

Later that year, he undertook a special mission to the province of Chiapas, where he appears to have accomplished notable work. A document in the Indian Archives at Seville narrates that he suppressed many abuses the Indians were suffering in that region, settled difficulties among the local governments of the pueblos, stopped frauds against the Royal Treasury, and out of his personal funds aided needy Indians.

This would indicate that he was not only Don Francisco's grandson, but had some ability and force; and that, within the limits of his background, class, position, and ambitions, he was not a bad sort—although the English friar Thomas Gage, who lived in Santiago de los Caballeros for several years and then wrote a somewhat nasty, though perhaps mainly truthful, book about the Guatemala of that period, records a remark by Don Luis to the effect that his position as a justice of the Audiencia paid him four thousand ducats yearly but, in addition, also offered him opportunities for "trading" and not unfrequent bribes, which presumably he did not scorn.

*The house is built on the Calle de
la Nobleza*

No KNOWN RECORD EXISTS OF EXACTLY WHEN
Don Luis de las Infantas Mendoza y Venegas
started to build the house on Primera Avenida,
or First Avenue, popularly called the Calle de la
Nobleza, the Street of the Nobility. But the likelihood is that, succumbing to the charming sur-
roundings of the Guatemalan capital and the
matchless climate, and deciding that his future lay
in the New World, he determined soon after his
arrival to erect a permanent home for himself.

[48]

The Centuries

The house was ready for occupancy by the end of 1634, following Don Luis' return from Chiapas —or (as this is written) slightly over three hundred years ago.

There was no regular architect or designer connected with the building of the house. No one person planned it. It was the collaboration of many men.

Wilson Popenoe, who has read extensively on house-building in those days, believes that after Don Luis de las Infantas Mendoza acquired the large corner lot—about one-fourth of a city block and most of it facing on the exclusive Calle de la Nobleza, not far from the great San Francisco church and monastery and even closer to the Plaza, with its Cathedral and the Palace of the Captains-General—he called together his masons, most of whom had been apprenticed in Spain, and discussed with them his future house. Or perhaps he conferred with just one of them, the Maestro, who was a sort of builder-contractor and also knew something about doors and window frames and grilles, and was probably authorized to hire and supervise the carpenters, locksmiths, and other artisans required for the job.

They surveyed the site, Don Luis and his men; possibly drew a few freehand lines on a sheet of paper, and the masons drove in several stakes to mark the numerous corners. They decided on the approximate height, length, and width of the zaguan and the corridors; the approximate size of the sala, the library, the several bedrooms; the general location of the kitchen, the servants' quarters, the bathroom, the privy, the horse stables, the pigeon loft; and the thickness of walls, the tiling for the roof, and the flooring for the rooms and the corridors. They discussed what other materials were needed, whether or not they were all available in Santiago or nearby . . . and then the Maestro and his assistants and helpers set out to build the house. It probably took them more than a year to finish it.

The masons were their own architects and designers as they progressed with the work. It was all very simple. The style of the house that Don Luis wanted was probably even more in their

blood and bones than in his. It came out of Spain,
and was almost organic with them. They, like he,
had brought it with them from Seville, Cordova,
Granada, Toledo. They were good, proud workmen: artisans: artists: the best type of person, at
least functionally, that came over in those days.
They contributed more lastingly to the New
World than most of their better-known fellow
colonists.

The rough, unskilled labor was done by Indians for little or virtually no pay.

Undoubtedly, young Doña Feliciana was con-
sulted by her husband before construction of the
house was begun. She could not differ profoundly
with his and the artisans' idea of what the residence of a man of Don Luis' position, quality, and
pretensions should be in Santiago de los Caballeros de Guatemala. Very likely she suggested a
few special details for housekeeping convenience
and greater elegance. When the house was finished, its main features doubtless closely resem-

[51]

bled those of her father's home on the Calle de Bayona in Seville.

Here were the same general forms, proportions, values, effects; only this house was a good deal more spacious than the average private dwelling in Spain. There was so much more room in this New World than Back Home. For this reason, houses were built in one storey. They spread out over extensive plots. But another reason for most of the houses being only one-storey—though never openly admitted—was the possibility of earth-quakes.

Here, under the brilliant, kind, tropic-highland sun, was this large quadrangle of rooms arranged round the conventional main patio—the latter as yet without any full-grown trees, but doubtless bordered with flowers or shrubbery and enlivened by a fountain. The rooms, all opening on the court, were capacious, especially the sala, which measured ninety feet in length and twenty-two in width. All the chambers had bright white-washed walls, high, beamed ceilings, tiled floors, paneled doors, and medallion windows with wooden shutters, also paneled. Four grilled windows in the sala faced on the street. The corridor roofs were supported by turned columns of durable cypress wood, set on chiseled stone bases.

Visitors arriving on horseback alighted in the cool, din zaguan whence the mounts were led through a smaller passageway on the left, also of gray stone and Moorish in design, to the stable, where the manger and the watering trough were both of stone.

The kitchen was approached from the main patio through a third Moorish passageway—on the southwestern corner of the quadrangle—which was almost as large as the entranceway, and thence by way of a small flowered patio with three exits, all leading to other courts. The kitchen itself was fit to be the interior of an oratorio, or small chapel. At one end, the domed chimney gave the ceiling above the hearth, which resembled an altar, a lovely vault-like effect. Near the middle of the room was a thick, low, slow-curving arch separating the kitchen proper from the servants' mess-hall. And, built into the walls on the other end, were two large dutch ovens with small iron doors, no less suitable for roasting beef, venison, ducks and turkeys than for baking bread.

In the bathroom, adjacent to the cookery, and with entrance from the kitchen patio, were two sunken tubs constructed of blue and gold tiles. One was large, for adults; the other tiny, for babies. Doña Feliciana could have bathed her infant in the small tub while kneeling or standing in her own bath; but, being a great lady, she probably let the maids do that. They possibly bathed her, too. Cold and hot water issued from tanks placed in the back wall connecting with the kitchen.

The privy was a little room adjoining the bath.

The pigeon loft, directly over the bath and the privy, was a low garret-like place with enough pigeon-holes to accommodate two hundred birds, and an oriel through which they could fly in and out. It was reached by a short, narrow stairway beginning in the small, non-Moorish passageway between the kitchen patio and the pila court, with

[54]

its great square stone trough, in which laundry-maids did their washing.

Another staircase, spiraling up a round, tight tower, led from the pigeon loft onto the azotea, a flat roof over the kitchen. From it one could gaze down into the remotest patio of the house which was given to a small, very formal garden with arriates, decorative masonry-bordered flower-beds, and a tiny fount yielding a trickle of water that fell into a small stone basin, shaped like a grape leaf.

From the azotea one could view also the patios of at least two of the neighbors, a great expanse of tiled rooftops, and the domes, cupolas, and bell-gables of the nearly two score churches of Santiago; the many hills encircling the town, with their fields, meadows, and oak and cypress groves; the great cones of the extinct Agua and the cease-lessly smoking Fuego; and—during the seven rain-less months—much blue, very blue sky, with here and there a white, sun-shot cloud.

The probability is that Doña Feliciana de las

Infantas, while occasionally deeply homesick for the more gracious and mellower atmosphere of her native Seville, and often uneasy about she scarcely knew what, was quite content to be the mistress of such a house.

What Don Luis had in mind just then

BASES EXIST—IN THE RUINS OF PRESENT-DAY
Antigua—for the belief that in the middle and
toward the end of the 1630's the Infantas home
had, in point of size and the architectural style
then most ardently admired by Spaniards, no serious rival among the private residences of Santiago
de los Caballeros—with one possible exception:
the Casa de los Leones, which, however, was not
on the Calle de la Nobleza, but six blocks away,
close to the town's principal shopping district.

The House in Antigua

It was so called from the two stone lions with curious human faces which stood—still stand today, although the house is in virtual ruin—one on either side of the imposing doorway. The owner was a certain Alvarez de las Asturias, unquestionably a bigwig of some sort, perhaps a well-to-do merchant.

The Casa de los Leones was built about a decade before the Infantas residence . . . and fifteen years subsequently, after the completion of the latter, the two houses became involved in a tragedy that shook the emotions of the Guatemalan capital almost as fiercely as the quake in the ensuing century shook its walls and roofs. But of this—which occurred when Don Luis de las Infantas Mendoza y Venegas no longer owned the house he had built—in due course.

For the time being, in the latter half of the year 1634 and through the early months of 1635, there was not the least hint of anything tragic or even unpleasant about this newest domicile on Calle de la Nobleza. Don Luis' future seemed as bright as the sun that flooded his patios.

Although but forty, he already held a very high and distinguished office. He was energetic, ambitious. He had initiative, daring, the skill of impressing himself upon people who counted. He was beginning to be generally regarded as brilliant, competent. Why else, one may ask, had he been the one selected to straighten out the difficult situation in Chiapas?

As a result of the success of that mission, Don Luis was now favorably known to the King and the Consejo de Indias in Spain and to the Viceroy in Mexico, who exercised general authority over the Guatemalan territories; and his position as a supreme court justice at Santiago de los Caballeros, which would have satisfied many another man, probably seemed to him more and more only a stepping-stone to higher posts and functions in the New World. For the New World—now that its "pacification" had been completed for several decades—was beginning to settle down to the business of being an empire and a civilization.

The House in Antigua

The Indian Question came to the fore every now and then, not only in Guatemala but in Mexico and Peru, as well as in the mother-land. Tens of thousands of indios had been slaughtered, but there were Spaniards, among them Don Luis de las Infantas, who realized the error of the old Alvaradan policy of murder and extermination. They wanted to make amends, so far as possible —and Don Luis may have thought that his future lay in the direction of what he had done in Chiapas.

Also, the work pertaining to the Indians interested him. It suggested an outlet for his abundant energy, curiosity, and love of adventure. The Indians were strange folk. Some inclined to be friendly in spite of all the brutality and injustice they had suffered this past century, and were still suffering, at the hands of the conquerors. To decent treatment they responded with a moving sweetness of manner. Privately Don Luis scoffed at the notion that the Indians were not fully human, that their souls were not immortal. He did not need the Pope's official opinion on that score. They were "inferior," to be sure; but they were also useful, willing and industrious—and more so when friendly than when sullen and hostile. They should be helped, won over, and made friendly.

Roughly, this had been the idea of occasional clerics—beginning back in the 1540's with the renowned "protector of the Indians," Fray Bartolomé de las Casas, son of a shipmate of Columbus—who had attempted to put it into effect and been invariably quelled as radicals or sentimentalists by the "realistic" military practitioners of force. But now that general conditions in Spain's New World were more or less settled the time might soon come for a laic or civil official to assume leadership in working out a practical and humane long-range Indian Program. And why could not and should not he be the man?

Don Luis de las Infantas' immediate problem was that of further building up his prestige.

Not unlikely, Doña Feliciana was a talented hostess, and as such no slight asset to her husband; and who can say that they did not build the splen-

did house on the Calle de la Nobleza mainly to
advance his career? Don Luis and Doña Feliciana
possibly planned social affairs while the home was
still in the process of being built. In this spacious
house they would entertain and impress the
King's and the Viceroy's inspectors and messen-
gers and other magnificos, civil, military, and ec-
clesiastic, when they came to Guatemala on their
official tours from Spain or Mexico. Else why the
great sala, so marvelously suited for large recep-
tions? It was the largest in any private home in the
city.

Why, too, the big pigeon loft? To raise birds
for their table? Unlikely. Far more probably, to
raise carrier pigeons. From such missions as the
one he had made to Chiapas one sent his reports
by them.

In many ways a typical Spanish colonist, Don
Luis de las Infantas was not a deeply contempla-
tive man. He was mainly incapable of complicated, sustained thinking. In common with every
other ambitious white man in the New World,

he was mentally and emotionally involved in endless surface excitements, which came too swiftly
to be regarded by any one with objectivity or
philosophic profundity. Besides, Spaniards generally were not thinkers or philosophers.

But—from what we know of him—it is more
than possible that off and on as the house was
being built, or when he and his family were already moved in, he uneasily queried himself just
how this dwelling differed, in other than architectural respects, from his native home in Spain.
What did it lack? . . . Home? When and how
did a house become a home? With the framing
of the union of two people, such as he and Doña
Feliciana, within some well-arranged solid masonry? Did children make a house a home? Was a
home an extension of one's personality? Did it
take Time—years, decades; births, deaths, mar-
riages—to turn a house into a home? . . .

These uneasy thoughts reached into his memory. Back home in Cordova he had had something
that nobody here in Santiago de los Caballeros de
Guatemala yet had. In Cordova, there had been

a warmth, a rhythm of life. Here life ran hot and cold, indeterminate. Nothing was fixed, definite. In Spain, there were tens of thousands of homes—that was the word for them: *homes*—in which the same families had lived for six, eight, ten, fifteen generations. Here in Santiago, few, if any, native Spaniards lived in the houses of their birth; while the recent immigrants or colonists, restless and unstable, also changed dwellings every few years, building, selling, buying, tearing down, building again.

No one yet *belonged* here.

No one felt deeply secure.

Why was that?

The Spaniards were the ostensible masters of these great regions, but there was in them the deep, seldom admitted fear of the Indians. Hence their policy of terror and brutality toward the aborigines. Or, at least, that was one of their extenuations for it. Those who feared wanted to fill with fear those they feared. This policy, ruthlessly practiced by men in high authority and their subordinates, gave the country an outward

aspect of peace and order; but actually it served
only to make this whole complex scheme of fear
worse and worse, and which could lead to nothing
good or sound in the long run. But how to put
an end to it? Was it all a vicious circle? . . .

Could a house become a home in these circumstances?

Don Luis himself was afraid. Was that why—at
least one reason why—he wanted a different, more
humane policy toward the Indians? He did not
like to be afraid. How much of his idealism was
to be ascribed to his fear of being afraid?

Deep within him, in common with everybody
else he knew in this New World, he had been uneasy and apprehensive from the first. He half-
admitted—only half-admitted this to himself, and
but for a moment. Like every one else, he and
Doña Feliciana were pretending otherwise. They
had been going through the motions of orderly,
elegant living. They had built this fine house in
the exact style of houses Back Home. One explanation of this, to be sure, was that they brought
the idea from Spain. But there was another ex-

planation. There was this Fear, formless but constant; it made some people almost frantic in insisting the masons adhere to the architecture of
the mother country in every respect. It represented a tangible tie to the reality of the past.
They wanted to live in a bit of Spain, which to
them, consciously or unconsciously, was synony-
mous with security and stability. They had a
profound need to emphasize this kinship with the
old country. He himself had this need to overcome the Fear, to keep it from invading his consciousness at all hours of day and night.

It can be assumed that Don Luis de las Infantas
realized, at least vaguely, that to the people Back
Home this form of architecture was attractive
chiefly for the reasons already stated—namely, because a house so built was a place of seclusion, a
mark of one's outward calm, a symbol of one's
austerity, a statement of one's disinclination to
exhibitionism, and so on. But he did not—could
not afford to—consciously and clearly admit to
himself that one of the highest virtues of a Spanish
Renaissance-Moorish dwelling in this New World,

which was so full of Conquest-created hate and fear, was that physically it looked so like a fortress. It gave one a feeling of safety—at least a superficial feeling, an illusion, of safety, of being home.

In common with other Spaniards in Santiago de los Caballeros, Don Luis de las Infantas was occasionally willing to admit to himself that the danger of earthquakes or of Fuego erupting was a reality here, and that it was for that reason foundations and walls must be made extraordinarily firm and thick; but—also in common with his contemporaries and equals in Guatemala—he did not admit to himself that potentially and in the long run the human situation here might prove to be far more pregnant with quakes, eruptions, and other disturbances than was the earth beneath his feet. He only dimly sensed this truth in the form of the tremor of fear which, although it ran through everything in Spain's New World, seldom even so much as touched the consciousness of responsible people, because they could not bear, nor afford, to think about it.

This thinking, by and large, was no thinking

at all. It was spasmodic reacting on the part of their fear instincts.

So it may be that the dynamic of Don Luis de las Infantas' ambition to get on in the New World, which led him to build a house that would be a means to advancing himself, was partly, if not principally (and, of course, for the most part unconsciously) fear, or, rather, the vague oft-recurring inner discomfort that fear produced in him. Holding a higher position, he might be able to do something toward a wiser policy concerning the Indian, and thus toward removing the chief cause of that fear; or, at least, he might be able to surround himself with more eloquent immediate symbols of safety.

Superficial talk at
the Bendición de la Casa

BUT, ALL THAT BEING AS IT MAY, IT REQUIRES scant effort to imagine that Don Luis de las Infantas' bendición de la casa, or housewarming, was what modern society reporters would describe as a "brilliant affair," to which "everybody" came. And "everybody" in Santiago de los Caballeros de Guatemala at that time—even from the meager information about them that has come down to us—were an interesting lot.

[69]

The House in Antigua

Among those who attended the housewarming, which probably began late in the afternoon and lasted till after nightfall, were very likely the new governor, who was also president of the Audiencia, and his wife; his grace the Bishop, who gave the place his official priestly blessing, and some of the archdeacons; the high-ranking officers of the garrison, the director of the Mint, the visitors from the homeland, and Don Luis' four fellow justices of the high court and their wives; the family from the Casa de los Leones, the alcaldes, and other important municipal officials. Also, the heads of the several schools, who were all ecclesiastics belonging to various Orders, but most of them, perhaps, not ill at ease in mixed society. Also, the two or three artists from Spain or Mexico who were in the city anonymously painting good, bad, and indifferent pictures of the Blessed Virgin, the Trinity, and Santiago and other saints for the churches and oratorios and the private homes of the well-to-do. Also, most of the big merchants of the city and the rich planters and hacendados from the vicinity with their wives and grown-up sons and daughters.

[70]

Among those present, perhaps, and, if so, much noticed by everybody but more especially by the men, was young Doña Juana de Maldonado de Paz, "the very fair and beautiful" daughter (so friar Gage described her some years later) of Don Luis' colleague, Judge don José de Maldonado de Paz. She was then not yet twenty. Subsequently, employing her youth and beauty and skill in music, she played havoc with the high laics and ecclesiastics of the city, and with the community as a whole, while trying—vainly, but falling very short of success—to become Abbess of the rich and powerful Convent of Nuestra Señora de la Concepción. On taking the veil of a nun, according to Gage, she "at her own charges built for herself a new quarter within the cloister with rooms and galleries, and a private garden-walk, and kept at work and to wait on her a dozen blackamoor maids . . . which," added the sarcastic friar, "was enough for a nun that had vowed chastity, poverty, and obedience."

If Doña Juana, or another equally entrancing woman or girl, was not present, there was prob-

ably interesting talk in various corners of the
sala and in the small biblioteca next to it, or—
if the night was balmy, as nights often were—
in the corridors and the patio.

Much of the conversation, no doubt, concerned
itself with the house and its appointments.

When evening came, scores of candles were lit
on the numerous candelabra and chandeliers in
all the rooms, and in the lanterns in the passage-
ways and the patios, enabling those who arrived
late to see clearly every detail of the place. The
guests, suppressing their envy and jealousy, admired everything, exclaimed at this and that, and
time and again congratulated Don Luis and Doña
Feliciana upon their taste.

The ladies took close and careful cognizance
of the style, fabric, and embroideries of one another's garments, coiffures, ear-rings, fans, scents,
size of waist, and bearing . . . and between these
scrutinizing glances may have chatted about the
Very Venerable Sister Berengaria, a nun of the
Order of Santa Clara, who was a subject of lively
discussion just then.— For twenty years Sister

Berengaria had been the humblest, most pious nun in the cloister, serving as cook, doing all the kitchen work and uncomplainingly attending to some of the lowest menial tasks outside the kitchen as well. Day after day, year after year, the good woman had been the first to rise and the last to retire, unaware that she had the love and respect of all the other sisters. Recently the Abbess had died and in the ensuing election Sister Berengaria, who had not even been a candidate, was unanimously elected to the vacant office. The poor soul had been beside herself when informed of her election, and doubly so when, according to a legend going the rounds of the city, seven of her predecessors in the office of Abbess had risen from their crypts in the church of Santa Clara and entered her cell to congratulate her! . . . The ladies half believed the legend.

The caballeros, or gentlemen, perfumed, manicured, wearing silk, velvet and brocade, and great ruffs around their necks and gold or jeweled buckles on their shoes, and the ecclesiastics in long, somber robes, almost certainly discussed the Indians; the latest newcomers from Spain; the news from Mexico City, Lima, Hispaniola, and the mother country; and the phenomena, trends, and developments at Santiago de los Caballeros and in other towns and villages of Guatemala.

A few copies of *Don Quixote de la Mancha* had lately reached the city from the homeland. Don Luis had read the first part of the work while he was still in Spain, but some of his guests, who had just perused it, discussed it very heatedly. This man Cervantes was apparently lampooning knighthood and some of the best attributes of the Spanish character. Who was he, anyway? A mere vagabond! He had applied for a position in America and been rejected. Good! thought some. Others opined that to have refused him a job had been a mistake. As a government official he might never have written such a book. . . .

Not improbably, some wonderment was expressed among the gentlemen concerning the fate of the English colonies in certain territories of North America, which were said to be extremely

cold and populated by aborigines far more dangerous than had ever been the worst of the
Quichés, Tzutuhils, Cakchiquels, Mams, Chujs,
Ixils, Choles, Chortis, Kekchis, and Pokonchis in
Guatemala. The Santiagans had been hearing of
those northern settlements for over two decades.
Was that place—what was it called? Jamestown or
something like that—*si, si,* Jamestown . . . was
it still in existence? Who could say? The probability was that all the settlers had long ago either
frozen to death or been slaughtered by the savages;
and neither would be surprising, for the English
lacked the true faith. They had allowed their
religion to be influenced and "reformed" by
preaching madmen; so God in retribution struck
many of them with madness and they were going
to North America to perish. . . . But it was
strange, was it not? that Jamestown was also named
for Santiago (St. James). . . . Well, the English
were welcome to the frozen wastes of North America! . . .

These leading men of Santiago pretended—in
their social talk—to be rather confident of them-

selves. Each tried to make all the others believe
that he had his feet firmly on the ground and was
gazing unflinchingly into the future, which one
could not discern clearly and far ahead merely
because it was so bright; and they were so good
in deluding one another that in the end they succeeded in deluding themselves.

The destruction of the first capital had long
since become almost a legend. True, the volcano
Fuego fumed incessantly and, every once in a
while, belched forth great volumes of fine ashes,
which spread over half of Guatemala; but that
was nothing. Everybody was used to that. There
had been no earthquakes worth mentioning for
ninety years, ever since the founding of this new
city of Santiago. Which palpably signified that
the Almighty God approved of the new site, and
approved of *them*, who were for the most part people of higher virtues and better education than
had been the conquistadores and the earliest colonists. Many of them owned, and occasionally
read passages from, Ignatius de Loyola's *Spiritual
Exercises for Overcoming Oneself and for Regu-*

lating One's Life Without Being Swayed by Any Inordinate Attachment. So was it not natural, then, to assume that, if He did not approve of their townsite and them, He would have destroyed the city long before this, as He had destroyed the first capital when it was scarcely ten years old? . . .

They believed, these outstanding men of Santiago de los Caballeros, along with the rest of the populace, or at least strived against disbelieving entirely, that the Almighty had demolished the original settlement mainly because He had been displeased with Don Pedro de Alvarado's widow, Doña Beatriz, who, mourning for him, had painted her house black, which was interpreted in Heaven as not mere mourning but a clearly disrespectful protest against Divine Will. The fact that Doña Beatriz had perished in the catastrophe supported this belief—which was one of many such views and opinions held by the best minds of that day in Spain's New World.

A serious quarrel
about something or other

S OCIAL AFFAIRS DOUBTLESS OCCURRED IN THE
Infantas residence during the months immediately
following the bendición de la casa, but not many
. . . and, likelier than not, some of the later ones,
were not especially "brilliant" or well attended.
For ill luck began to pursue the owner of the
splendid new house, and it was not long before
the structure of his ambition and ideals collapsed.

Early in 1635, Don Luis received news of his

father's death in Spain, and promptly applied for
leave from his post so he might go home to settle
the estate. He asked two of his relatives living in
the Old Country to intercede for him with the
King and the Consejo de Indias and urged that
the request be granted to him without delay.

It was never granted.

Sometime in 1636, while his application, en-
tangled in leagues of red tape, was still going
through the official channels in America and in
the Old Country, Don Luis de las Infantas Mendoza and two other justices of the Audiencia got
into deep and long-drawn-out trouble with the
governor of Guatemala, Don Alvaro de Quiñones
Osorio. There was a most serious quarrel. It was
put before both the Consejo de Indias and the
King. But what it was about, the known documents—which are replete with references to it as
"the Quarrel of Santiago de los Caballeros de
Guatemala"—do not tell.

The dispute concerned, perhaps, the question
of policy toward the Indians. Or the governor, as
president of the Audiencia, might have attempted

to usurp the traditional power of the other members of the Court, and these three judges—possibly led by Infantas—objected. Or the majority of the court wanted to curtail the authority of the Executive. . . . Quien sabe?

Possibly it was all a matter of personalities. Conceivably, the clash revolved, at least in its inception, around Don Luis de las Infantas and his fine new house. The governor, perceiving that the young justice was in the grip of ambition, deemed it necessary to check him. He might have been envious or even afraid of Don Luis. One thing led to another. A surface issue was created. Or it sprang out of the antagonism. This issue produced others, more fundamental. Two of his fellow justices sided with Infantas, and the governor, as the supreme officer of the province, possessing certain disciplinary power, restricted all three to their respective dwellings, except that he allowed them to "walk the shortest route" to and from their offices twice daily.

"The Quarrel," which must have held the attention of all Santiago, dragged for two years

. . . until the King, in Spain, finally determined that all four, the governor and the justices, had behaved in a manner ill befitting their high offices, and fined the former a thousand ducats and the latter five hundred each.

Then, in 1638, the King returned Judge Infantas' application for leave without approval, and Don Luis was informed that if he so wished he was free to depart from his post and go home. Nothing was said about holding the position for him, and he seems not to have gone to Spain to settle his father's estate.

Details now become scarce.

We can be certain, however, that "the Quarrel" did the career of Don Luis de las Infantas Mendoza y Venegas no good. He continued as a justice of the high court for a while longer, but, having been involved in a bitter controversy which had called forth Royal displeasure, he was more or less to be shunned. Few people came to the fine house on the Calle de la Nobleza. No important person entered it. And the envious and the I-told-

you-so's, many of whom had attended the bendición de la casa, were secretly, or even publicly,
gleeful that it was so. It served Infantas right! He
had aspired too high. He should have been satisfied with the justiceship. It had been presumptu-
ous of him to build so noble a house, and on the
most exclusive street in town, after but two years
in the country, and he hardly forty.

Here we can indulge in a few second-thoughts
about Infantas. Like most ambitious men, he was
a complicated, ill-integrated person: a liberal, a
progressive, an intellectual, a dilettante, a poten-
tial picaroon; a bit of everything, nothing very
definite. Pulled in various directions, his energies
could never achieve full function or realization.
He was, perhaps, very much like millions of men
nowadays who in youth seemed promising, about
to do something or get somewhere, but who are
nowhere. The world is against them, or so they
think; and to an extent they are right. The world
was against Don Luis de las Infantas.

During the years of "the Quarrel" he must
often have paced about in the patio of his house,

blinking at the bright sun, pulling at his beard
(he doubtless had one) ; then, with a sigh of resig-
nation, entering one of the cool, dim rooms. He
did not feel at home. His house, but——

He was confused, miserable, perhaps sorry he
had built the place.

Under these circumstances, Santiago de los
Caballeros and the province of Guatemala as a
whole became intolerable to him, to say nothing
of the effect these developments had on Doña
Feliciana: and in 1640, after either resigning
the justiceship or having been relieved of it, Don
Luis was holding a curious position in Mexico.
It included collecting taxes on pulque and other
beverages and managing, of all things, the government playing-card factory.

After this the archives, both in America and
Spain, are silent about him till 1682, when he
died in poverty in Mexico at eighty-seven years
of age. Doña Feliciana had evidently died before
him. Following his death, their children were returned to Spain as pobres de solemnidad, "re-
spectable paupers," at the expense of an uncle.

The House in Antigua

The last known document in which Don Luis de las Infantas' name occurs is the application of his oldest son Nicolas, then in his late forties, petitioning the King for a pension in recognition of his father's services in the American colonies.

Meantime the house on the Calle de la Nobleza was acquiring a history of its own.

"The servant of
God" tinkles his bell

ON HIS APPOINTMENT TO THE POSITION IN
Mexico, Don Luis de las Infantas sold his fine
property to his erstwhile fellow Oidor de la Audiencia, Don Teófilo de Alvarenga, who there-
upon owned it for the rest of his life, till 1652—
for twelve or thirteen years.

During that period, having been built and
owned by one judge of the supreme court, and
having passed into the possession of another, the

house commonly began to be called the Casa del Oidor.

During that period, too, Don Teófilo's wife died, and his daughter, Doña Beatriz, who had moved into the house as a child of six or seven, grew up into a young lady of rare beauty and talents.

Beatriz had many suitors, but was most responsive to the courting of young Don Alvaro de las Asturias, son and heir of the owner of the aforementioned Casa de los Leones. Her father, however, who was an arrogant man, violently disapproved of the youth. He wanted her to marry someone else; whom, it is unknown. No doubt he considered the son of a merchant beneath the level of a judge's daughter, especially *his* daughter. Or it may be that he did not want her to marry at all while he was alive. There was need for a mistress in his own household. He was too old to remarry.

One morning in 1651 the body of Don Alvaro

de las Asturias was found in a clump of aloes behind the church of San Francisco. He had been
stabbed to death. The crime shocked and mysti-
fied the city. Robbery, evidently, had not been
the motive; for nothing had been removed from
the boy's person.

Some months later the mystery was penetrated
by a curious young man who had come to the
Guatemalan capital only the year before, and in
that brief time become one of the city's best known
and loved figures.

This young man was Pedro de Betancourt, born
about 1625 of a well-to-do and favorably known
family of French descent in the town of Tenerife,
Canary Islands. He was mainly uneducated but
possessed a deeply religious nature, permeated
with a great and active love of mankind, especially
the poor.

At twenty-four—perhaps after some sharp and
profound disappointment in his home city—he
abruptly decided to go to the New World, of
which he had been in almost constant awareness

since boyhood: for many America-bound ships passed within sight of the Canary Islands, some stopping there.

When he reached Habana, the young man got off the ship and, strolling about, chanced upon the mooring-place of another vessel, which he learned had cargo consigned to Santiago de los Caballeros de Guatemala. He had not heard of this city before, but the sound of its name affected him strangely. "I was filled," he told later, "with an inward joy and great strength urging me to proceed thither."

Soon after his arrival in Santiago, he was accepted into the brotherhood of the Third Order of the Franciscans and given the title of Hermano, but after a while became popularly known as Hermano Pedro. His superiors, however, regarded him at the beginning as a very dubious asset to the brotherhood, for he had an extremely poor memory and was incapable of learning by heart the long formal prayers he was required to recite in church. This made him very miserable.

Hermano Pedro lived in solitude for a period, fasting, praying (no doubt very informally), occupying himself with the contemplation of divine things, and letting the true light illumine his spirit. Presently he acquired a thatched hut somewhere on the periphery of the town, formerly inhabited by an Indian, and turned it into an institution that was a hospital for the poor, a school for their children, a place of worship, and an all-around asylum for the afflicted and the weary.

He had a dark-brown beard and receding hair that matched the color of his dusty friar's robe; people called him "the Servant of God," and he rapidly developed a devoted following. He had no difficulty in raising funds, and persons of all classes came to him eager to enter the service of his cause. He soon had a larger stone building near the church of San Francisco for his school and hospital, and the nucleus of a society which he—being exceedingly fond of the story of the birth of Christ—named the Congregation of the Bethlehemites.

The House in Antigua

Up and about day and night, Hermano Pedro scarcely ever slept or rested. He was a two-legged ambulance, calling for the sick and bringing them to the hospital on his shoulders, regardless of whether they were Spanish, Indian, or of mixed blood. He was the doctor, pharmacist, head nurse, cook, teacher, and priest.

His regular diet was dry bread and water, with an occasional bit of fruit. When weariness laid its hand on him so firmly that he no longer could sit, stand, or keep his eyes open, he would murmur a quick, informal prayer begging the Lord to forgive him his limitations, and lie down wherever he happened to be—in the street, on a country road, in a field, under a tree, in someone's courtyard, anywhere—and permit himself a wink of sleep.

Nights, when there were no other duties to perform, he walked the length and breadth of Santiago de los Caballeros, tinkling a little bronze bell, and calling out in a deep voice to all who would hear his admonitions to confess and repent their sins, to pray for the dead in Purgatory, and to come to the aid of the poor and ill.

When the corpse of Don Alvaro de las Asturias was discovered, Hermano Pedro was already an institution in Santiago de los Caballeros . . . and some weeks after the murder, which was still the main topic of discussion, he began to make it a point during his admonitory nocturnal rounds of the city to pause near Judge Alvarenga's house on the Calle de la Nobleza and, tinkling the little bell, to emphasize the "confess and repent" part of his call.

Hermano Pedro kept this up, always waiting awhile by the portal of the great house, until one night Don Teófilo came out, haggard and trembling, and begged the young friar—he was then not yet thirty—to conduct him to his cell. He wished to confess a great sin and ask his counsel.

The next day Don Teófilo appeared in the chamber of the Audiencia without his judicial robes and, addressing his colleagues on the bench, confessed to having hired a half-breed to kill his

[91]

daughter's suitor, and asked them to judge him as the actual murderer. He did not disclose the name of the half-breed, who he insisted had been only his tool and was innocent.

For a week after the news of this confession had spread through the city no work but the most urgent was performed by anybody. Judge Alvarenga, the aloof and remote Don Teófilo, always wrapped in the aura of his office, father of the beautiful Beatriz, was in prison for the slaying of his daughter's beloved! Would the other justices of the high court sentence him to the gallows? Could a judge be executed like any other criminal? Hanged? Would not the King be called upon to decide in the case? . . .

And Doña Beatriz! What would she do now? Who would marry her, a murderer's daughter?

The girl wept inside the splendid house on the Calle de la Nobleza while on the cobblestones outside stood hushed crowds, their quiet intermittently pierced by hysterical sobs and cries. The tall grilled windows facing the street were closely shuttered; the great door was bolted within; no one came out.

The Audiencia sentenced the confessed murderer to the gallows and on his own urging he was promptly hanged in the spacious courtyard of the Palace of the Captains-General. All that day half the town stood on the great Plaza before the Palace, silent or weeping, mostly silent; while over the valley vibrated the sound of more than a score of church bells tolling in desperate confusion.

A few days later Doña Beatriz de Alvarenga entered the convent of Santa Catarina situated not far from the house where she had grown up, but even closer to the Casa de los Leones; and she assumed the name of Sister Teresa.

The crime and the punishment were remembered and discussed in Santiago de los Caballeros for decades afterwards. In fact, every once in so often the episode is mentioned in local conversation to this day.

[93]

The House in Antigua

But now—in Antigua—the affair is usually recalled only in connection with Fray Hermano Pedro, who, enfeebled by his labors and self-sacrifice, died in 1667 (of which more in a moment) and a century later—not long before the great earthquake—was canonized, and now remains buried in one of the ruined edifices, where the poor, the ill, the sore, the wretched come daily to pray before his crypt.

How did Hermano Pedro know that Alvarenga was the real murderer? The theory is that some time following the crime the half-breed had come to him and confessed to having killed the youth at the behest of Don Teófilo, whereupon the friar concentrated his nightly admonitions on the judge until he confessed too. They then decided that Alvarenga should immediately confess before the Audiencia as well and suffer the consequences.

An extraordinary tenant—
Don Rodrigo de Arias Maldonado

BESIDES THE UNFORTUNATE DAUGHTER, DON Teófilo de Alvarenga left also one or more sons, who at his death became co-owners of the house with Doña Beatriz; thus she could not deed the property to the convent, which doubtless she would have been inclined, if not required, to do, had she been the sole owner.

If any members of the Alvarenga family continued to live in the Casa del Oidor after the exe-

cution of the judge, there is no known record of
the fact. In all probability it was sold soon after
the tragedy, or offered for rent, or both.

In 1666 a dashing, wealthy young bachelor, Don
Rodrigo de Arias Maldonado y Velasco, scion of
one of the leading noble families of Granada,
arrived in Santiago de los Caballeros de Guatemala from the sub-province of Costa Rica. Although but thirty years of age, he had lately occupied the position of governor of that province
with such "distinction" that he was now generally
regarded as the foremost of Spain's younger
colonial administrators. In Costa Rica he had
been known as a man of great rigor, especially
in dealing with the Indians; but apparently he
came to Guatemala for relaxation and pleasure,
and, according to one of his biographers, "opened
a great house and lived in lavish style, taking a
prominent part in the activities of local society."

The "great house" was the Casa del Oidor.

Don Rodrigo de Arias Maldonado, however,
was a tenant in it for only two or three months.

Soon after his arrival he received from the King papers bestowing upon him the title of Marques de Talamanca—in recognition of his "brilliant" subjugation, a few years previous, of the Talamancan Indians in Costa Rica. This promptly caused the people with whom he associated in the Guatemalan capital to address him as "Marques," and there was popular talk of the virtual inevitability of his becoming in time Viceroy of Mexico or Peru.

He was one of those darlings of fortune whom both men and women envy without malice and cannot help admiring and being drawn to, even when not fully approving of all their actions, creed, and criterions. There was an irresistible, infectious vitality about him. Even when silent, he seemed to be communicating something to all about him. He was tall and broad, with a dense red beard that glistened in the light. A natural man, he had a singular, effortless personality. He was not ambitious, yet progressed to positions of ever increasing importance. He *was*; things happened about, with, and to him. And whatever happened seemed right, inevitable. He belonged in the Casa del Oidor, and he imparted to the house a brief radiance it had never known.

No one begrudged him his new title.

He did not immediately acknowledge the receipt of the Royal papers—almost certainly because at about the same time he fell deeply in love with a beautiful young woman who was the wife of an elderly official of high rank.

One night he stole a few moments with the lady in her house while her husband was absent from his home, and she, overcome with emotion, died in his arms.

Horrified, Don Rodrigo de Arias ran into the street, wanting to blurt out the awful truth to the first person he encountered. But the hour was late and the streets were deserted.

Nearing his own dwelling, he heard the tinkling of Hermano Pedro's little bell. He had seen and heard about the bearded, dusty friar before this. Now he ran to him and, breathless, began to tell him what had happened. But the Bethlehemite placed a gentle hand over his mouth and, insisting upon silence, bid him come to his cell.

They spent the night together, talking and praying. By dawn the rich and brilliant cavalier, the erstwhile terror of the Talamancas, was a changed man. To say that he had come completely under the influence of the poor, shabby friar, would be inaccurate. He simply became a person with a new rôle and function in life, entirely different from what he had been and done.

Don Rodrigo de Arias returned the high title to the King, explaining in his letter that, on a sudden, worldly honors had ceased to have meaning for him; and he became a brother of the Congregation of the Bethlehemites, exchanging poverty and abnegation for his gay and proud career.

This, naturally, caused as great a sensation in the whole of Santiago de los Caballeros as had Don Teófilo de Alvarenga's confession of murder fifteen years earlier. The abrupt turn in the life of the great gallant was discussed in tones and terms of intense curiosity and awe. For a time only he, Hermano Pedro, and a servant in the lady's house knew how she had met her death. The secret was not disclosed until later. The people of the city imagined she had died of one of the several usual causes of sudden death, and that Don Rodrigo, whose love for her had been whispered in the city, had become a Bethlehemite out of pure grief.

People spoke of him as "El de la juventud borrascosa—he of the wild youth." But no one understood him. And there was not much about him that lent itself to comprehension. He seems to have been one of those individuals who in the space of an hour live more than do most people in a lifetime. His career was meteoric, dramatic, intensely full and satisfying. Such as he either die at the peak, which occurs in youth, or early in life undergo a complete transformation. Their lives have no gradual, painful dimmings; no slow, sordid decline. Like synthetic dramas, they have swift climaxes, which are promptly followed by abrupt, glowing sunsets. . . .

At this time Hermano Pedro was only forty,

but, while still a force spiritually, he was nearly worn out physically. The ensuing year put him upon his deathbed, from which he commissioned Fray Rodrigo de la Cruz, as the late gallant now called himself, to make the Congregation of the Bethlehemites "great for the Glory of God" with "branches in many parts of the world."

In his new life, Fray Rodrigo attained to a ripe old age and, being a man of action, established numerous hospitals and diverse other institutions for the poor in Peru and Mexico, and a few in Europe.

He lives in the consciousness of Antigua to the present day . . . but, like the crime and punishment of Teófilo de Alvarenga, mainly in connection with Hermano Pedro.

A successful man—
Captain Lorenzo de Montufar

Dᴜʀɪɴɢ Dᴏɴ Rᴏᴅʀɪɢᴏ ᴅᴇ Aʀɪᴀs Mᴀʟᴅᴏɴᴀ-
do's brief tenancy, the Casa del Oidor was doubtless the scene of a number of social affairs that surpassed in "brilliancy" the early Infantas parties.
And their brilliancy was different. Don Luis had
meant to use his house for political purposes, and
his parties were in consequence more or less
strained with secret ambition on his part. Don
Rodrigo's suppers and "evenings" were free, natural, without purpose apart from themselves.

[102]

But when this gallant turned a religious, the house once more passed into decline; and, so far as is known, nothing very stirring or beyond the conventional happened there for decades after.

Almost simultaneously with Don Rodrigo's dramatic encounter with his fate, there arrived in Santiago de los Caballeros from Spain a young army officer, Captain Lorenzo de Montufar, accompanied by his wife and two children. He was not devoted to military life, not poor nor well-to-do, but sharply cognizant of material opportunities in the New World and bent on taking advantage of them and improving his economic and social status.

The Montufars could not afford on arrival to buy or build a dwelling, and there was a great scarcity of houses for rent. The population was increasing, and there was a general housing shortage. So, when Don Rodrigo suddenly vacated, they took the Casa del Oidor—it continued to be known by this name.

The Montufars probably wondered why they got so noble a residence so easily and cheaply.

Newcomers that they were, they had not yet heard of a vague superstition the city was developing about the house—that there was a curse upon it. First, its builder, Don Luis de las Infantas Mendoza, had been smitten by ill luck; then its second owner, Don Teófilo de Alvarenga, had met the worst imaginable end; and now Don Rodrigo de Arias——

When finally the Montufars heard of the superstition, it was too late for them to change their minds; they had, to all seeming, signed a contract equivalent to the modern lease. But, so far as known, they never regretted having taken it. Installing themselves in it immediately after Fray Rodrigo de la Cruz had moved to his cell in Hermano Pedro's institution, they avoided misfortune through all the decades they lived in the house.

Captain Montufar left the military service soon after he arrived in Guatemala and went into business—into several businesses: trading with the homeland, Mexico, and the West Indies; into farming, lumber, local merchandizing and municipal politics, which he doubtless manipulated to the advantage of his other pursuits. He was shrewd, aggressive, and opportunistic; a materialist; a man of no great virtues but many petty ones; a cross between Marco Polo and Babbitt, with a touch of Otto Kahn; competent and successful in all, or most of, his enterprises.

After occupying the Casa del Oidor as a tenant for a year or two, Lorenzo de Montufar bought the property—in all likelihood for a low price. Then he lived in it for over thirty years, till his death, a prosperous and respected man in a city rapidly expanding in size and importance. During his time building boomed. Such great churches and institutions as Escuela de Cristo and Santa Teresa were erected, and Montufar probably furnished some of the materials at substantial profit.

He became not only one of the wealthiest but one of the most solidly popular and influential men in the city. A pillar of society. A contributor to charities. A public character. A patron of the arts, he was one of the first laymen in Santiago de los Caballeros to have his portrait painted— it is now in Wilson Popenoe's possession and presents Montufar as a slight man physically, with a thin, sharp face that has a kind of cunning self-righteousness, tempered by a trace of good-will.

Montufar was elected an alcalde of the city four times and, finally, alderman for life. Of his wife nothing is known except that she bore him several healthy children in addition to the two who had come with them from Spain.

Their descendants are now scattered through various parts of Guatemala, not a few of them occupying prominent positions in the country's business and political life. On the modern railroad between Puerto Barrios and Guatemala City there is a station called Montufar.

After the Montufar family had lived in the house for a few decades its name was changed to Casa Montufar. The superstition about its being a home of ill luck had ceased with most people long before that. Others believed that Don Rodrigo had broken the bad spell on it with his renunciation of the world, and that the Montufars

fell into a barrel of good luck simply by happen-
ing to follow him in the occupancy of the house.

How long the Montufars owned it, is unknown,
but it seems they held title to it well into the first
quarter of the eighteenth century, when the son
of the late Lorenzo de Montufar and his family
moved to another house—very probably because
the old dwelling, now approaching the ninetieth
year of its existence, was no longer safe to live in:
for early in that century Santiago de los Caballeros de Guatemala was badly shaken by a succession of earthquakes, which damaged together
with many other buildings the Casa Montufar.

The earth beneath the city heaves and trembles

For a hundred and ten years after the founding of Santiago de los Caballeros the region between the two volcanoes suffered no earthquakes. In 1657, however, a severe temblor greatly frightened the inhabitants and damaged slightly a few churches, civic buildings, and private residences.

Then all was quiet again till the last half of the 'seventies, when—in 1676 and '79—two light

shocks occurred, causing pots, vases, and candle-
sticks to topple over. No worse were the two jolts
in 1681 and '83. They, however, were followed
by two "heavy" quakes in 1687 and '89, which
loosened the tiles on some of the roofs and cracked
several walls in various parts of the city.

The next quake, also "heavy," occurred in 1702,
and did considerable damage. Then peace once
more beneath the earth, till 1717. . . . But in
these fifteen years Fuego erupted eight times, dis-
charging volumes of ashes.

The year 1717 was until then the worst in
Spanish memory with dozens of bad heaves and
shocks, and Fuego erupting again intermittently
and voluminously for weeks at a time, obscuring
the sky so that the sun was a faint red disk and
the moon a pale glow behind the murk. This,
of course, added to the terror of the people, and
a sect developed around the idea that the end of
the world was nigh. Others believed that the world
might last awhile longer, but that the city would
soon be completely destroyed; God was displeased
for a number of reasons, and it would be best to

abandon the town and start a new community somewhere else.

By now only some of the newest and stoutest structures were wholly undamaged.

The Montufars abandoned their house about this time.

In the ensuing thirteen years the earth under the valley of Panchoy gave not a twitch or shiver. The rifts in the walls were more or less repaired throughout the city and the world's end ceased to seem imminent even to the most fearful and superstitious Santiagans, while those who held that God was angry at the city became less urgent in advocating the transfer of the capital.

Above the valley, the yellowish fumes issuing from Fuego were thin and faint, often barely discernible from below.

Then, in 1730, the earth indulged in another spasm and most buildings in town were cracked once more. From many of the houses roof-tiling fell in pieces. Here and there entire roofs, supported by worm-eaten beams, collapsed, crushing to death a number of persons. Brief shakes followed at intervals of two or three days, a few extremely severe—which doubtless resulted in new cracks in the walls of the house on the Calle de la Nobleza, now untenanted and for sale.

After the first earth-heave the people congregated in the streets and the patios. The whole town was near panic. Most of the churches and congregations conducted all-day processions, which met one another at street-crossings, and there were scenes of fear-inspired religious hysteria. Shocks occurred during these solemn parades and people were hurled to the ground by the invisible forces under their feet, or they threw themselves down in helpless consternation. Men, women, and children knelt day and night in the patios and on the cobblestones outside their dangerous dwellings, praying at the top of their voices, burning incense and sprinkling holy water.

The crowd in front of the Cathedral moaned in unison when a shock clipped off a wing of an angel that stood high up in a niche near the bell-gables. Men and women then yelled and screamed as though that wing represented the worst of the calamity and they feared that the fall of the entire angel might mean the end of everything.

The provincial governor of Guatemala at this time, and as such the most important man in this situation, was General don Francisco Rodriguez de Rivas. He had been in office for several years and was an experienced administrator of cool, rigid intelligence and a character tough as whitleather. He more than suspected that earthquakes were natural phenomena, rather than manifestations of Divine Wrath or crude suggestions from On High to transfer the city to another locality.

Next to him in importance was Bishop Juan Bautista Alvarez de Toledo, whose character also was no soft or brittle affair. He held, doubtless in all sincerity, that these heavings of the earth certainly were warnings from Above. In His inscrutable wisdom, God *did* want the capital of Guatemala moved from Panchoy Valley, for the city *was* to be destroyed. He, the bishop, had had a premonition to that effect. Wherefore his Grace demanded that his Excellency forthwith command the abandonment of the present site and the removal of the entire population to another region —where to, the bishop himself had no idea or suggestion of one.

Determined to resist hysteria, Don Francisco Rodriguez de Rivas flatly disapproved of the demand. He granted the possibility, even the probability, that the city might be partly or completely destroyed at any time in the future, next week, or next year, or a hundred years hence; but he maintained, also, that the same thing was liable to occur in any other place they might select.

The governor scoffed at the bishop's premonition and came close to heresy when he argued that earthquakes were natural happenings caused by convulsions in the bowels of the earth, which were a matter not of sudden or momentary Divine displeasure with mortals or places but of contracting and expanding forces, which, in turn, might have some connection with heat adjustments down below. He did not doubt that volcanic

[113]

eruptions were manifestations of the same subterranean forces as earthquakes, and that in these Guatemalan highlands, as in other parts of the world, nature was apt to get violent at any time.

These two views resulted in an intense political battle, which added greatly to the panic.

The bishop's idea, more easily understood, found support in two of the principal nunneries, a few of the lesser male congregations, and perhaps the majority of the poor folk of the city; while nearly all the men of property, the military, and—most important—the Dominicans and the Franciscans, which were the richest and most powerful Orders, owning, or holding liens on, the best real estate in and around the town, sided with the governor.

The struggle between the governor and the bishop had scarcely begun, however, when these chaotic circumstances lifted into sudden prominence a third person who for a time pushed into the background the other two.

This was Juana Ocaña. The contemporary

[114]

chronicles of these events refer to her as mujer ilusa; we would call her a female crackpot. She wandered through the nerve-wracked community, haranguing the people. The tremors and rumblings of the earth signified that the valley of Panchoy was to be inundated and become a lake! All must flee, else they would drown and go straightway to Hell—if for no other reason, because of their current heedlessness of God's warnings!

Active partisans of the bishop's idea subtly encouraged Juana Ocaña to foment trepidation and hysteria . . . and soon frightened folk began to move into the hills and neighboring valleys, where they had no, or very inadequate, shelter for that time of the year, which was the middle of the rainy season, and many became ill and died.

The demented woman forecast the very day—October the fourth—on which the city would sink out of existence. As the date neared, the exodus increased. Others who believed her, some apparently too scared for flight, hastened to priests to confess their sins and to prepare for death.

A severe quake in the afternoon of the third of

October lent strength to Juana's prophecies, and more than ever was Santiago de los Caballeros de Guatemala sundered on the question of whether to move or stay. The scoffers scoffed more fiercely; the others demanded more shrilly that the governor forthwith employ military force to evacuate the city by midnight.

Most families had members in both camps. The majority of men sided with the governor; nearly all the women with Juana Ocaña and the bishop. That more people did not desert the city that night was because of this difference of opinion within families. Wives and daughters could not leave their stubborn, unbelieving husbands and fathers to perish alone!

That night in Santiago de los Caballeros was one of the craziest in the history of the human race. No one slept. Tens of thousands milled in bewilderment in the Plaza, knelt in the middle of the streets and patios, wept and shivered, and prayed in hoarse voices. Children cried and dogs yelped and squealed through the gloom. It rained intermittently. Several persons went insane.

The Centuries

The atmosphere was so completely one of fear and madness that some of the hitherto staunchest adherents to the governor's view abruptly swung to the bishop's and Juana Ocaña's side, and bundled up a few belongings and covertly fled with their families to the hills. Soldiers required to keep order deserted their posts and followed the refugees.

The fourth of October, however, was a calm, clear, sunny day. But for the usual streak of yellow smoke issuing from its crater, Fuego was a picture of peace; while Agua, whence the awful flood was popularly expected to come, was as placid as it ever had been since the destruction of the original Santiago de los Caballeros. In the evening the moon shone brightly and all the stars appeared in their proper orbits.

And October the fifth dawned as a fit successor to October the fourth.

Attired in his most brilliant official uniform and mounted on his finest horse, Don Francisco Rodriguez de Rivas rode through the city all day, preaching calm, and he regained the confidence of a good part of the population. Within a few days the life of the town was almost normal.

Juana Ocaña was summoned before the Inquisition, which by then had developed into a considerable institution in Spanish America. She was tried and sentenced to have her hair cut off and henceforth to appear in public clad in black.

But she continued to be a prominent character and a potentially dangerous person; so the governor contrived to have her confined to a cloister. She started to weep the first day she got there, then wept for the rest of her life, and she became known as La Llorona, the Weeping One.

Two months later a Royal decree came from Spain commanding the capital of Guatemala to remain where it was.

Then followed two decades of complete tranquillity.

The house is sold to the only bidder

To WHOM THE MONTUFAR FAMILY SOLD THE damaged house on the Calle de la Nobleza is unknown. Nor have we any definite knowledge as to who lived in it during the second quarter of the eighteenth century. Unsafe for occupancy, it may have stood empty for a long time. But Wilson Popenoe now has in his possession a voluminous and beautifully written document which shows that in 1738 the owners of the house were an

[119]

elderly couple named Don Tomás Sampeir de Herrera and Doña Teresa Cárcomo de Herrera.

In that year these two people were in some difficulty, and, hoping to alleviate it, they promised to give to the Monastery of Santo Domingo four hundred pesos. Such a promise to a great monastery in those days was a legal debt, and they were required to put up the house as collateral.

In the following years, however, the Herreras' affairs went from bad to worse. They were unable to fulfill the pledge, and in 1750 the Monastery sued them for payment of the amount. The case dragged for five years. Then the Audiencia ordered the house put up for auction so the debt might be liquidated.

This court order was promptly executed—in 1755—but the house was apparently in such poor condition, due to the earthquakes and subsequent neglect, that the auction attracted only a small crowd.

When the public auctioneer struck his gavel and called for bids, a captain of the Guards named Diego de Guerra, a resident of Santiago de los Caballeros, raised his hand and announced he

was ready to give sixteen hundred pesos in cash
and, by damn! not a centavo more. In his opinion
that was all the property was worth, and anyone
who offered more was a fool. (All this is min-
utely described and quoted in the document now
in Wilson Popenoe's possession.)

Disregarding the captain's last remark, the auctioneer called for further bids, but none were
forthcoming. "Then," he said, "if no one raises
this offer, *one—two—three*—it is well, it is good:
let the bidder take the property."

Diego de Guerra stated before witnesses that
he obligated himself to make his offer good.

A few days later he paid the sum in full. Five
hundred and thirty-six pesos were duly turned
over to the Monastery for payment of debt and
interest; thirty pesos went for court costs, and the
balance to the attorney for the defendants in the
case—but he kept most of it.

Captain Diego de Guerra, of whom little more
than has been told is known, took possession of
the house in 1761; repaired it, and lived in it
with his family—apparently—till the fateful year
of 1773.

The city is finally destroyed and abandoned

WHEN SAMUEL ADAMS WAS BUSY PRICKING THE English colonies of North America with his revolutionary pen, the inhabitants of Guatemala's chief city numbered about sixty thousand. This included twelve or fifteen thousand Indians, mostly Cakchiquels; while perhaps a like number of them, interspersed with a few hundred Spaniards and mestizos, lived in the tiny mud-and-cane hamlets and settlements and upon the fincas and haciendas within an hour's walk of the town.

[122]

The Centuries

The new Palace of the Captains-General, the city's most imposing structure, occupying the entire south side of the broad Plaza, had been completed in 1764, and the vast church and monastery of Merced four years earlier. The great period of Spanish Renaissance-Colonial architecture, however, was over. In point of basic architectural and esthetic values in church-building the Merced was inferior to the older edifices.

And the city generally was not what it had been, or had promised to become, a hundred years previously. There was, to be sure, the new University, the third institution of higher learning on the American continent; and there was the printery, the second in the Western Hemisphere; but the intellectual and cultural life of the city was neither high nor brilliant. Indeed, it was rather paralytic.

The Jesuits, who were the most sagacious and aspiring among the priesthood, had been expelled in 1767, along with all the members of their Order in Spain's New World colonies. The command for the expulsion had come from Charles III, who had been influenced by the anti-Jesuit drive in

Europe. Among the banished Jesuits was Rafael
Landivar, a native son of Santiago de los Caballeros, educated in Italy, who is reputed to have
been Guatemala's greatest poet. His chief work
was *Rusticatio Mexicana,* a long poem in classical
Latin. He was also a great conversationalist and
wit.

In recent times there had been several epidem-
ics, which had taken some of the best people in
the city and left most of the worst. Men and
women were worn out, and inertia and vague
despondency prevailed.

And there had been more earthquakes. True,
these had not been severe, but one never becomes
used to earthquakes.

Social and economic conditions could not have
been more deplorable. In the preceding hundred
years, the great monastic Orders—especially the
Dominicans and the Capuchinas—had gradually
come into the possession of most of the valuable
property in the community and the best farm
lands surrounding it. The Indians' status on these
properties was poorly disguised slavery, but the

[124]

situation of thousands of lower-class Spaniards and mixed-breeds in the city was almost as reduced. Most of the wealth was used for great new bronze bells and gold-leaf altars, for paintings and statues of saints and the Blessed Virgin, for golden candelabras, enormous prism-glass chandeliers, and other elaborate and costly decorations in the churches.

The Indians and other poor people lived, at best, on the hope of Reward in Heaven. Hundreds of them stood in queues in monastical courtyards, waiting for the nuns or monks to give them scraps of food.

Numerous families, however, were departing from Guatemala for Mexico, Peru, or the various islands of the West Indies, where economic opportunities were not yet so circumscribed; or were returning, disappointed, to Spain. During the 1760's, the town's Spanish population had decreased by some five thousand.

In the early 1770's, there were few wealthy families in the city. The Montufars were one. The Asturiases another. Their riches were derived mostly from indigo, cowhides, tobacco, liquid amber, and balsam, which were exported to Spain. But their fortunes, too, were on the decline.

The numerous small shops, depending largely upon the patronage of government employees who numbered less than a thousand, were not doing well. The masses lacked money to spend for anything but the merest necessities, if that.

Perhaps four-fifths of the city lived from hand to mouth. Hunger and general wretchedness prompted an increasing number of persons to petty crime. The two prisons in the city were crowded.

As the colonists of North America started their War for Independence, there were in Guatemala vague beginnings of a cautious anti-clerical sentiment. On Sundays and holidays and even on occasional weekdays people filled the nearly two-score large churches and the numerous smaller houses of worship, and were generally God-fearing Christians and Catholics, going to confession and communion; some of them, however, whispered among themselves that the good fathers belonging to the various Orders might be mistaken. The Lord probably did not want these new golden bells and golden candelabras, great chandeliers and magnificent altars, nor this huge new church of Merced, while men and women, His children, were destitute. And some were quite sure the Blessed Virgin of Succor in one of the large edifices did not care for the string of more than a hundred pearls that had lately been adoringly wound around her neck.

Prophecies were again uttered that the Almighty would soon indicate His displeasure with this situation in no dubious way. The extreme radicals, who were not numerous but articulate, went so far as to suggest that the sooner He did something about it the better. A small but growing sect again began to believe that the world's end was scheduled for no far future.

On the whole, however, the inhabitants of Santiago de los Caballeros were ill prepared for 1773.

Light earth-shocks occurred in March and April

of that year. On June nineteenth, there was a terrific rainstorm punctuated by brief subterranean roars and jolts, which, however, caused only slight damage.

Followed ten days of clear, warm weather and perfect calm.

Then, at twenty minutes to four o'clock in the afternoon of June twenty-ninth, a quick, sharp quake drove everybody who could move into the streets and the patios. There was a standing government ordinance—superfluous, no doubt—requiring people to vacate their dwellings as quickly as possible whenever the least quake was felt.

For the next ten minutes everything was still. The very air was motionless.

Numerous persons knelt on the cobblestones in the middle of the streets, praying. Others, who had grabbed the holy-water vessels on the way out, sprinkled the walls of their habitations from a safe distance.

Then—at ten minutes to four—commenced the longest and severest earthquake in the history of the city. For fully a minute the earth shuddered and waved, heaved and jerked. The crashing of collapsing houses and churches throughout the city stunned the ears of the panic-stricken people, so that few heard the accompanying underground rumble.

Thousands of men and women, unable to stay on their feet or knees, sank to the ground, which shook, foundered, and buckled under them. Those who could keep their eyes open in spite of the clouds of dust saw walls fall, roofs cave in, tile hurtle through the air, and trees jumping out of the ground with their roots. Cobblestones flew up from the streets as though catapulted, and hit people. The church bells still in their gables clanged by themselves, but their spasmodic tolling could scarcely be heard through the clatter and din of the catastrophe.

All in a heap, the city was a cry of agony.

Such large and elaborate structures as the Cathedral, the former Jesuit monastery and college; the convents of Santa Catarina, the Capuchinas, Nuestra Señora de la Concepción, Santa Teresa, and

Santa Clara; and the Santo Domingo, Franciscan,
Escuelo de Cristo, and San Augustin monasteries
and church edifices were almost totally destroyed.
The Palace of the Captains-General was half
ruined. Least damaged was the architecturally ob-
jectionable Merced church; no doubt because it
was new and its walls were extremely thick and
had not been weakened by previous quakes. The
new university was also little damaged, for the
same reasons.

Save for a few of the most recently built, all
private homes were demolished. In many instances not a wall remained intact. The Casa de
los Leones was about three-quarters ruined.

This was approximately true also of the house
that the ambitious Don Luis de los Infantas Mendoza y Venegas had built so hopefully on the
Calle de la Nobleza not quite a hundred and forty
years earlier. Of this once so fine a dwelling only
the kitchen structure, with its superb vaultlike
chimney, strong arch, and baking ovens, stood undamaged.

Because most of the inhabitants had sped outdoors at the first shock fewer people perished than one would expect in so great a catastrophe. The number of dead was one hundred and twenty-three, and these were mostly old and sick people and young children alone at home when the destruction began. A few died because the initial quake had not been powerful enough to rouse them from their siesta.

Two women were buried by falling roofs while in labor.

This astonishingly low number of victims, however, does not include the many who died of fright during the minute-long shaking, and of injuries subsequently. The hurt crowded toward the Hermano Pedro de Betancourt Hospital, but this old institution, too, was in ruin.

Among the dead were also several prisoners. Four hundred of them had escaped when the walls of the jail collapsed. No one bothered to apprehend them. People even helped to free them of balls and chains.

Scores of people went utterly mad seeking for their wives, husbands, and children. Hundreds were mildly deranged for the rest of their lives.

The House in Antigua

Nearly everybody prayed, for by now most people firmly believed that this horror was but the prelude to the imminent end of the world. It would be senseless to try to leave the scene. One had best prepare oneself to face the Judge. Priests sat on the ruins of their churches confessing people, who knelt or stood in long queues and made no secret of their sins. Waiting for their turn with the confessor, the sinners—some in silks and velvets, others in rags—confessed to one another. They addressed fervent cries to "the merciful God," the Blessed Virgin of Succor, and the saints.

Life-long enemies clasped each other tearfully. Thieves returned stolen property, when it was possible to salvage it out of the ruins; or they confessed to their victims, who, out of sudden good will, readily forgave them. Couples who had been living in sin married hurriedly. Common agony and the imminence of the Final Cataclysm made everybody equal and brought out the best in most. Everybody forgave and helped everybody else. Rich Spaniards kissed the hands and faces of poor Indians whom they had been abusing and exploiting for years.

Equality in helplessness seemed to fortify people. Fear turned to pity, prostration became strength.

This continued all the rest of that day and that night and into the morning of the next day.

When the Final Cataclysm failed to occur, however, the populace gradually regained some of its normal faculties, opinions, manners, and attitudes.

Children wailed and adults realized that they, too, were hungry, and that the thing to do was to rise from their knees and go foraging for something to eat. There was a food crisis, for victuals were buried and destroyed in the ruins and the Indians of the villages on the surrounding slopes were too frightened to come down with the usual supplies. Those who found anything to eat hoarded for themselves and their families.

The dead were threatened by zopilotes and had to be buried. Thieves took to thieving again. Some of the former enemies resumed their mutual hatred. The escaped prisoners decided it would be expedient for them to leave the town.

Indians began to be treated as before.

Some one ventured to estimate that the damage amounted to more than forty million pesos. Others began to wonder if the city was worth rebuilding.

The government commenced to function again. Committees were sent into the country for food, which was then rationed. A semblance of order was restored. Pillagers and marauders were shot or cut down.

All except three or four baking ovens of any size were destroyed, and two of these were in the kitchen of Captain Diego Guerra's otherwise ruined house on the Calle de la Nobleza. They were intact. The government commandeered them, and for a week or two most of the bread eaten in town was baked there.

In the second half of 1773 and early in '74 a few more shocks were felt, but they were slight.

Then complete calm.

The Centuries

And now the old fight was renewed. To move or to rebuild? The issue split the town into two parties, and the struggle continued for three years. The big convents and monasteries, with their vested interest in lands and what walls remained of their buildings, were for staying and rebuilding. In this they were supported by other property owners, except those whose holdings were heavily mortgaged to the Orders.

But in the end the big interests lost out. In 1775 the King of Spain ordered the removal of the capital to the Valle de las Vacas, also known as the Valley of the Hermitage—the present site of Guatemala City—and the ruined town became known as Antigua.

The building of the new Guatemalan capital was begun in the year in which the people of North America, having declared their independence, started to create a new nation.

And, ironically enough, beyond a few faint tremors now and then, Antigua has not had a quake since, whereas the new capital of Guatemala has been shaken several times—and in 1917 was half ruined!

The poor and lowly take over Antigua

WITHIN FIVE YEARS AFTER THE DECISION TO
create a new capital had been reached, some four-
fifths of the population of Antigua moved to the
distant Valley of the Hermitage, which, like the
first two sites, was one of great scenic beauty, with
high cone-shaped volcanoes round it, but which
was less protected from the winds, more change-
able in weather, and therefore a trifle less agreeable climatically, than were the valleys of Almolonga and Panchoy.

[136]

The Centuries

This removal of the Guatemalan capital was one of the most interesting migrations in the history of the Americas—and an extremely arduous one: at least for those who effected the actual physical transfer of the movable property belonging to the Government, the Church, the business and professional groups, and the private families and individuals. These movers were almost entirely Indian and half-breed cargadores, or burden-bearers.

As birds fly, the distance between Antigua and the new site was not great, eight or ten miles; but the trail connecting the old city with the new location tobogganed up and down so many deep barrancas and over and around so many hills and mountains that the walking distance was about twenty-five miles. The loads that were strapped upon the skulls and backs of thousands of these human beasts-of-burden weighed from one to two hundred pounds, and, although about one-third of the trail had grades between ten and twenty degrees, they were required to make the trip in not more than two days.

The entire governmental personnel moved,

with their archives, seals, and inkpots; and the bishop and the religious orders, male and female, moved with all their detachable wealth, including the less damaged altars, statues, vestments, holy-water founts, books, candles, snuffers, and other tools and adjuncts of the Roman Catholic religion.

The big merchants moved, and nearly all the petty shopkeepers and many would-be business-men and upstarts who visioned the opportunities that were certain to develop in the new city.

And preceding, accompanying, and following the upper and middle classes were between thirty and thirty-five thousand workingmen of diverse grades, trades and categories, and their wives and children. Many of these went because there was need of their skill and service, and they were arbitrarily ordered to go; others because they knew that, with an entire new city being built up from bare ground, there would be no end of work— hard work, and ill-paid, to be sure; nonetheless, an opportunity to function, to live.

About a thousand well-to-do ex-residents of the

former Santiago de los Caballeros, weary of earth-quakes and tired of ruination, quit Guatemala for other Spanish provinces in the New World, or returned permanently to the homeland. Like the propertied people who left for the new site, these emigrants abandoned their damaged or demol-ished houses, indifferent or resigned to what might happen to them or to Antigua as a whole.

The rest of the population—some eight or ten thousand men, women and children: about half of them Spanish, the other half Indian and mestizo —remained in Antigua.

These were mainly the very poor, the lowliest, the untrained, the least resourceful, the mendi-cants, those unburdened with Spanish pride, the most wretched and incompetent, or so seeming, whom nobody wanted, cared about, or was able to use.

A kind of municipal government, with a small body of troops, and one or two priests were left in the ruined city, but in the hurry and bustle that went with the inception of the new capital no one of consequence felt any responsibility for, or interest in, the stay-behinds. They could do what they liked. They could shift for themselves.

They did—and most interestingly.

Families and individuals moved into the abandoned ruins having the most solid walls, and erected temporary grass roofs over their heads . . . and there they lived, those who did not die of something or other; or at least they existed, ate and slept, and had children . . . and within a decade or two Antigua was a strange but orderly community.

One man opened one kind of shop in his ruin; another, a different kind in his. One made an attempt at carpentering or shoe-making, another at masonry or wood- or ironwork. A number of families got together and cleared a section of the great Santo Domingo church-and-monastery ruin and started to grow vegetables and to raise pigs and chickens. Another group installed a few looms in a section of the former Capuchinas' monastery where the roof remained, and took to weaving.

And so it went.

Within a decade following the catastrophe, and

[140]

especially during the rainy season, tall and lus-
cious grasses grew all through the vast ruins of the
Franciscan church and monastery, as well as in
other great ruins: and what could have been more
natural and sensible than for sheep and cattle to
be driven in for pasture?

Indians from closeby settlements came to town
with produce, and the great old Jesuit establish-
ment, what was left of it, with its roofless walls and
spacious courtyards, was ideal for the main communal market-place.

An enterprising soap manufacturer opened a
factory in the sacristy of the church of La Recolección. When business increased, he spread out into
a wing of the church proper that still had a roof.

A one-time patio of the same ruined edifice was
used as a corral, while the skeleton of the Santa
Rosa church became a superb cow barn. The
ruins of certain other houses of worship were
turned, respectively, into a mattress manufactory,
a slaughter house, a tannery, and a cartshed.

What occurred in Antigua was similar to what
had come to pass, some thirteen centuries earlier,

in the immense Diocletian Palace in central Dalmatia, where—after the death of the great Roman Emperor who had built it, and after invaders had sacked the nearby villages—homeless peasants occupied the Palace and kept life, work, and trade going within it until it became the heart of what is to-day, the largest, most thriving city on the eastern Adriatic shore. . . .

With this organic social-economic process in Antigua, the town's municipal government inevitably improved, for disputes and problems which had to be dealt with arose. Sanitation was more or less taken care of. A few churches were partly restored.

By and by Antigua was made the seat of authority for the entire region beneath the Fuego and Agua volcanoes.

And, simultaneously with all this, those people of Guatemala City who had abandoned their properties in the old town again became interested in their ruins. They still held titles to them. So, in many instances, they sold them to the new inhabitants for whatever was offered; in others, they began to charge rent.

The rents, to be sure, were not very high: between ten and thirty cents a room monthly, for the majority of the tenants were, naturally, still very poor. Only the "well-to-do" among them turned over ten or fifteen pesos a year in actual money.

But one could live on that, and marry and raise a family—except that in Antigua few bothered to marry in order to raise a family. The two or three remaining priests, who were also poor men, charged too much for the marriage ceremony, even if it was only a handful of coppers. So most young people merely paired off and lived together and produced offspring. No one worried about racial "purity" or racial "integrity." As poor people living in a town of exclusively poor people, they had no such ideas or concepts. Simple and free, they were all more or less equal.

They were Hermano Pedro's folk. The late friar may not have had a very bright mind, and he had only recently been canonized, but to them he was the greatest of saints, a hero. His old hospital, just west of the Franciscan ruin, was restored and by and by a doctor came from somewhere. And when they felt a need to pray, these people of Antigua went to Hermano Pedro's crypt, which had not been damaged, although the church wherein it was built into a wall was a ruin.

The result was that during the first century after the final destruction of the city, or between 1775 and 1875, the Spanish and Indian races in and around Antigua became rather thoroughly and naturally fused and amalgamated . . . and before long the predominant type in the ruined city was a handsome, graceful person with a light-brown skin, a friendly smile and disposition; not ambitious or aggressive, but inclined to do just enough to get along, or less—and that was little enough.

For a considerable length of time, perhaps well over a hundred years, while they all remained poor and unaggressive, none of them cared what they were, Spanish or Indian. They regarded themselves Antigueños. Some went so far as to denominate themselves Guatemaltecos.

With the dawn of the nineteenth century Guatemala became an independent and very small country, but in all probability this made precious little difference to the average man or woman in Antigua.

If measured in human happiness, this—from the late eighteenth to the late nineteenth century—was perhaps the best period of the city since its inception. Individual human lives were not on a very high plane, but they had a basic vitality, strength and tone; while the chief element of communal life was friendliness. There were no social ambitions and pretensions, no impositions, no intense desire for possessions; little fear; no keeping up with the Joneses.

There was much simple beauty, of which no one was very aware; it was part of the organicness of one's daily life.

People laughed much—at and with one another, at themselves. There was endless amused criticism of their circumstances. Here they were, poor as

could be, but living in palacios on the Calle de la
Nobleza, their shops in great edifices, grazing cattle in church naves, and raising pigs in sacristies!
It was funny when one thought of it—a Joke which
God had played on Himself and reduced to their
understanding, so that they could share not only
His Pain but His Humor and Laughter. The essential drollery of the situation crept into the people's unconscious and created in them a lively
sense of humor. Everybody was somewhat of a
jokesmith or practical jester. Everybody had a humorous nickname. And not a few were proud of
these popular appellations. Their quips and jokes
were not lacking in slyness or even wit. Nor in
realism. They were given, more or less, to ridicul-
ing themselves and their circumstances. But at the
same time they developed a kind of unconscious
philosophy, which might be stated thus: If you
live in the face of Destruction and do not run
away from it, you win over it; you become im-
mune against fear; you need no longer be a bluf-
fer, a whistler-in-the-dark; you can be, you must
be, you *are* humble; you are free to laugh—you

had to laugh, you laugh, for life, in part, was a
Joke, at least here in Antigua.

As one decade followed another, not a few of
the houses were more or less restored, at least to
the extent that they did not appear as ruins from
the streets, which were also cleared of most of the
débris. And the ruins as such improved by themselves, or, rather, Time and the elements, especially the torrential rains during the five-month
wet season, smoothed and polished them off. Trees
began to grow in the erstwhile rooms, and diverse
and sundry vegetation found foothold in the
cracks and crevices of the walls. Fungi, mosses, and
ferns softened the reflection of the sun's glare on
old masonry.

Great sections of walls and arches looked as
though they might tumble down at any moment,
but stayed where the earthquake of 1773 had left
them, decade upon decade.

In the last quarter of the nineteenth century,
however, the old town commenced to change
somewhat. Aggressive individuals came from

Guatemala City and converted large sections of
the valley of Panchoy into coffee plantations;
coffee was planted in the ruins, wherever there
was room for a couple of trees; and Antigua became a bit of a business center. Some of the poor
went to work as coffee-pickers for from ten to
twenty cents a day; some sold themselves to the
planters into virtual slavery; and—almost imper-
ceptibly—the general character and outlook of the
people was altered.

Yet the curious old city retained much of its
charm and appeal.

But to return to the house on the street once
known as the Calle de la Nobleza.

As already suggested, the great old dwelling,
owned by Captain Diego Guerra when the earthquake occurred, was not completely destroyed.
The main outside corner had been thrown seriously out of plumb, but most of the outer walls
and a few of the inner ones, though all badly
cracked, stood up. Except for the sections over the
wholly undamaged kitchen and the pigeon-cote,

the roof was down, and the rooms and corridors were piled with débris; on the other hand, the main zaguan and all the other arched passage-ways, connecting the various patios, were in fairly good condition. Yet, on the whole, the place seemed a hopeless mess, a worthless ruin; so, in common with every one else in this predicament, Captain Guerra had abandoned his property and followed his fortune to Guatemala City.

Three decades later, however, when Antigua appeared to insist on remaining a human community, his son, Tomás Guerra, developed a sudden and lively interest in the place, made a trip to the old city, and found several families living in the ruins to which he held title. He tried to collect back rental, but failed; then sold the property to some one whose name is illegible in the existing record of the transaction.

During the nineteenth century several people may have owned these ruins; but who they were is unknown. The paper used for official documents in Antigua during that time was of a poor grade and has since mostly crumbled. Certain it is, how-

ever, that the owners were persons out of the mass
of poor, plain humanity.

About the year 1850, some one planted a young
Capuchin cypress in the center of the main patio.
It grew rapidly, and twenty years later, because of
the tree's prominence, the ruin began to be called
Casa del Capuchino.

At approximately the same time, the main
patio, heaped with débris on which people could
sit, became a favorite arena for cockfights, which
had developed into a popular pastime in Antigua.

In 1870, one José Ruiz owned the ruin. He and
his wife, Gregoria Ruiz, lived in it with several
of their tenants, who were all poorest of the poor.
He died in 1880, leaving the place to his widow.
She tried to live on the two or three pesos that the
tenants were supposed to pay her monthly, but
had a difficult time of it. The payments came most
irregularly; she would not evict a tenant if she
could have, and she could not, for that was not an
Antigua custom: and what good would it have

[150]

Antigua and Agua

*Ruins
of
Antigua*

A Woman of Antigua

Exterior of the House;
in the distance, volcano Agua

Maria at the Entrance

Main Patio,
from the Entranceway

*The Cypress and the Roof,
with Hills about Antigua*

Corridor along the Sala,
leading into the Library

The Sala

Entrance to the Sala

Corner Window in the Sala

Library, with a Glimpse of the Sala

Fireplace in the Library

*Library Window and Door
from the Patio*

*Main Patio
through a Library Window*

The Fountain

Roofs of Antigua,
with a Glimpse of the Kitchen Patio

*Roof Terrace with Chimney
and a View of Agua*

Main Bedroom

Bedroom Corner

Details of a Bedroom

Wilson Popenoe's Bedroom

Mirror in a Bedroom

Small Bedroom

The Kitchen: One End

The Kitchen: the Other End

Cargadores

Arturo Santis, Master Mason;
Jorge Benitz; Julio Gomez, Woodworker

Wilson Popenoe as agricultural explorer in Ecuador in 192
above, Dorothy Hughes Popenoe, shortly before her dea

Casa de los Leones

*Ruins
of
Antigua*

done to throw a tenant out? The next one would have been no more successful in meeting his obligations.

The woman died in 1915, but shortly before that a man named Ciriaco Peralta, a bookkeeper with a sugar firm in Guatemala City, with whom she had become acquainted, helped her so that she did not die of extreme want; and in payment and gratitude she willed him the ruin.

It was Señor Peralta who sold the Casa del Capuchino to Wilson and Dorothy Popenoe.

Part Two
THE RESTORATION

A "true botanist"—also a pioneer

WILSON POPENOE IS OF OLD FRENCH-Hu-
guenot stock.

Jean Papineau (the name was thus spelled
then) came to America from Dijon, in 1687—or
about the time the Montufars owned the house in
Santiago de los Caballeros de Guatemala. He settled in the French Huguenot colony of New
Rochelle, New York. His grandson, Peter Popenoe, followed Daniel Boone to Kentucky, where
he was killed by the Indians.

Wilson's grandfather moved to Kansas. His father spent part of his early adult life as a mining man in Central and South America, and then returned to Topeka, Kansas, where Wilson was born.

In short, the Popenoes were a family of restless pioneers.

All along the line they had a strong horticultural bent which in some of them amounted almost to an instinct and a passion. In fact, Wilson's father, Fred O. Popenoe, was the first of them with whom horticulture was not a lifetime interest and occupation.

In 1905 the Popenoes moved to Southern California and settled on several acres of land at Altadena, a suburb of Pasadena. Here the family instinct, which was already active in the thirteen-year-old Wilson, asserted itself also in his father.

In Central America Fred Popenoe had become familiar with various tropical fruits; now one day in 1907 he brought home two seedling avocados he had picked up somewhere in Pasadena, and he and Wilson planted them. Neither of the seedlings, as Wilson now puts it, "amounted to anything," but they sufficed to give father and son a passionate and sustained interest in the avocado.

While Wilson was still attending Pasadena High School, he and his father were in touch, personally or by correspondence, with numerous would-be avocado-growers in the subtropical regions of the United States, with successful avocado-growers in Mexico and Central America, and with Doctor David Fairchild, head of the Division of Foreign Seed and Plant Introduction in the Department of Agriculture at Washington. By 1910 a number of promising avocado trees were scattered through what is now regarded as the Los Angeles area. Not all of these were either the direct or indirect result of the Popenoes' enthusiasm; there is no doubt, however, that the father and son were among the earliest, most important pioneers in avocado-growing in the United States, which since has developed into a vital industry in Southern California and Florida.

Young Wilson Popenoe met many Southern California plantsmen, professional and amateur, and his passion for botany and pomology deepened and widened. But the avocado remained his primary interest.

While yet in his teens, if he chanced to hear of an avocado tree somewhere in California, no matter how distant, he went to look it over and make notes on it. To do this, he often had to walk long hours, for motorcars or buses were scarce then, and his purse was slim, while the Southern California electric railway system was not nearly as developed as it is to-day. . . . And I suppose that the eager, almost nervous, and withal warm manner, which was one of the first things I noticed about him when we met in New York twenty-five years later, is to be traced in part to his youthful pomological enthusiasm. It is the manner of a seeker and finder, a scientist driven not by mere abstract or academic curiosity but caught in the grip of the great creative pioneer urge, that constitutes the elemental motive force of human progress. . . .

Not distant from Altadena was Pomona College, and it was inevitable that when Wilson

The Restoration

Popenoe went there in 1910 he would enroll for the botany and pomology courses offered by Professor Charles Fuller Baker, who had recently come to the college after working several years in Cuba and Brazil, and believed that Latin America as a whole was an incalculably rich field for the plantsman who was also somewhat of an explorer and adventurer.

And now, looking back upon his career, it seems also inevitable that after college, with the avocado still his main interest, and having the restless Popenoe blood in his veins, young Wilson should almost immediately become an explorer for the United States Department of Agriculture. The only thing he did before that was to take—with his brother Paul, now a prominent biologist in California—a trip around the world, one purpose of which was to bring back date palms from Arabia and North Africa.

The great Swedish botanist Linneaus had said, "Botanicus verus desudabit in auguendo amabilem scientiam—the true botanist will sweat in

advancing his beloved science," but Wilson Popenoe did not need this admonition. He was innately
driven to all manner of botanical effort and his
avocado fanaticism drew him to tropical lands,
where opportunities to perspire were constant and
unlimited.

Doctor Fairchild, his chief in the Department
of Agriculture and a rare kind of government official, understood the young man and turned him
loose in the West Indies and in South and Central
America to "hunt" for avocados to his heart's
content and to keep his eyes open for other fruits.
He gave him a free hand, and—except for occasional periods of duty in Washington, D. C., California, and Florida—Wilson Popenoe "hunted"
from 1914 to 1925.

The avocado—which, of all the less-understood
fruits, seemed to have the best possibilities for development in the subtropical sections of the
United States—was Popenoe's principal interest
during the years of his service with the Department of Agriculture. But he studied also the
Brazilian navel orange, the bananas, the mango,

[160]

the chirimoya, and scores of other South and Central American and West Indian fruits, which he then—1920—described in his *Manual of Tropical and Subtropical Fruits,* still the best book on the subject, used in horticultural classes of several educational institutions in Florida and California.

He discovered new plants, which were named after him. *Dahlia popenovii,* believed to be the ancestor of the modern cactus dahlia, he found in Guatemala; *Passiflora popenoei,* a passion flower, in Ecuador; and so on.

Engaged in these explorations and studies, he traversed every Latin American republic, except the Argentine, Uruguay, Paraguay, and Venezuela. Many of the countries he visited a number of times, and he explored them up and down, crisscross, from border to border. In slightly more than a decade he traveled, on a rough guess, between one and two hundred thousand miles, and not a few of these on foot and by muleback and cayuco; which afforded him endless opportunities for seeing out-of-the-way places, hidden, little-known regions of beauty, and for coming in close personal contact with people of all breeds and classes, including numerous tribes of Indians.

Speaking fluent Spanish, he was eager to understand whatever he encountered and, if possible, to be helpful. He was one of those rare Gringos whom the natives describe as being not at all like Gringos, which is a commentary on the majority of Americans (and other foreigners) in South and Central America, who have the tendency to look askance at the natives, crack jokes at their problems and political upheavals, abuse native labor if they have the chance, or never learn Spanish—as in the classical case of the man in Colombia who said, "I've been around here now for five years and none of these people here yet understands me when I talk!"

By the early 1920's Wilson Popenoe was one of the best known and best liked Americans in South and Central America. His papers on tropical fruits were translated and published in Spanish. He wrote a number of popular articles for *The National Geographic Magazine* and some less widely circulating American periodicals. His comings and goings were noticed in the press of the various capitals. Finally, as already mentioned, the University of San Marcos in Lima bestowed on him an honorary doctorate.

And Wilson Popenoe, in turn, developed a deep affection for the several South and Central American countries he knew best—but reserved his highest enthusiasm for Guatemala: and, in Guatemala, for the old ruined city of Antigua.

The world's best avocados grow in great varieties in the highlands of Guatemala, between four and ten thousand feet above the sea level. They were cultivated there by the ancient Maya nations and were one of their principal foods. To this day entire tribes of Indians subsist largely on avocados and corn.

So Pop spent several months each year in those high, cool-warm regions and usually made his base in Antigua—partly because an excellent race of avocados highly suitable for cultivation in California was very abundant thereabouts, and partly also because of the fascination that the old town held for him. He liked the people of Antigua, who, by and large, in spite of the new forces playing on them, were still among the most charming anywhere in the world.

He would spend three or four weeks in the hills hunting for suitable avocado budwood, which he then shipped to the States, there to be distributed gratis by the Government among the would-be avocado-growers; after which he returned to Antigua, to write his notes and reports, and experiment on himself with sole or preponderant avocado diets. Then, his work done, he prowled amid the ruins, which were interesting not only architecturally and archæologically but botanically: for, as already mentioned, all manner of plants grew in the cracks of the walls—or just out of walls even where there were no cracks. It was all very curious. Also, this region was rich in a great variety of orchids, which the natives cultivated in the patios of their dwellings, or grew more or less haphazardly in the ruins.

Pop never tired of rambling through the ruins of Antigua.

The Restoration

One Sunday, out for a stroll after lunch, he passed the Casa del Capuchino on Primera Avenida: only he did not know the house was called that. To him, it was just one of many unrestored ruins.

A burst of shouting within caused him to glance in through the open door and down the long zaguan, stacked high with broken old corridor columns and roof-beams; and he saw that a cockfight was in progress.

Pop went in.

Here was a large patio with weeds, brush, and cacti growing around and over great piles of débris, which rain, the centuries, and human feet had pressed and pounded down so they had the appearance of having always been there. Mice and lizards darted about. Several people crouched in a circle, jabbering excitedly among themselves, watching the cockfight.

Pop did not care for that. In the center of the patio, however, he noticed the great Capuchin cypress: a glorious tree, growing out of the dump-heap, surrounded by this ruin, which was inhabited by no one could say how many families.

The House in Antigua

He strolled out of the Casa del Capuchino and turned back to the boarding-house where he was staying. He had to finish his report on the latest batch of avocado budwood he had sent to the States.

But, walking to his lodging, he thought to himself that that *was* a handsome cypress, no doubt about it. And thereafter, whenever he passed the Casa del Capuchino, he stepped into the patio to look at the tree. . . .

A young woman comes from England

EVER TRUE TO THE LINNÆAN RULE ABOUT
perspiring for botany, Wilson Popenoe, just thir-
ty-one, spent the summer of 1923 in Washington.
In the temporary absence from the United States
of Doctor Fairchild, he was acting chief of the
Division of Seed and Plant Introduction.

One day his friend, Mrs. Agnes Chase of the
United States National Herbarium, telephoned
him. A young woman named Dorothy Hughes

[167]

had just come over from England. She was twenty-four, had been with the Royal Botanical
Gardens at Kew for five years and in that time
become an authority on Stipa, Panicum, and a
number of other genera of African grasses; she had
written papers in the *Kew Bulletin* about them.
The probability was, said Mrs. Chase, that Miss
Hughes would presently become connected with
the National Herbarium; but in the meantime
she needed employment. Could he give her a temporary job?

Mrs. Chase was so keen about the immigrant,
of whom he had been remotely aware before this
as an English authority on African grasses, that
Pop asked her to send the young lady over to see
him.

"Love," wrote Franz Werfel somewhere, "is
nothing more than the capacity for passionately
developing the picture of a human being in our
inner dark-room."

Wilson Popenoe had had the picture developed
before the girl came along. Thirteen years later

he told me that the minute she entered his office he knew—"I just knew"—that is how he talks: simply, directly, in quick, eager little spurts—"I just knew that she was the one I'd been waiting for—looking for—for a long time."

He was an idealist in regard to women; here was the ideal.

Fortunately, the ideal, on her side, had been looking for him . . . and, to make a short story no longer, the result was a case of love at first sight.

Born in Ashford, Middlesex, Dorothy Hughes was the daughter of a Welsh civil engineer. She attended the Welsh Girls' School, which was in her home town, till the war broke out; then, barely fifteen, went into "land work," or war farming; but, after a year of overworking herself, she suffered serious internal injuries that made her a near-invalid until 1918.

On her recovery, Dorothy studied botany at the University of London. Progressing rapidly, she became a student assistant in the famous botanical gardens at Kew, and within a couple of years impressed all who came professionally in contact with her work—although, as it turned out, she was not a natural-born and inveterate botanist. Shortly after coming to the United States, as it will appear more fully in due course, she gave up botany completely for other work, and never missed it.

Not beautiful in the Hollywood sense or magazine-cover sense, Dorothy Popenoe was a deeply attractive young woman: tiny but compactly made, vivid, intensely alive, quick, vigorous; sometimes too vigorous for her strength. What most people first noticed about her were her lovely complexion and melodic speech.

She and Wilson Popenoe were married four months after they met.

In 1924 the young couple went to Peru, and, as Pop had hoped she would, Dorothy fell in love with Latin America. Whereupon, seeing that she would be happy in the tropics, he decided to accept the position of agronomist with the United

Fruit Company, which in the course of years had been repeatedly offered to him.

The new job promised him greater opportunity for work in his field and, in addition, an economic future better than the one he could count on if he continued in the Government service. He hoped that eventually, after knocking about for a few years and seeing places, Dorothy and he would more or less settle somewhere. Perhaps in Antigua: who could say? They both wanted a large family, and would need a base.

In 1925 they moved to the United Fruit Company's port-town of Tela, in the Republic of Honduras.

*The agricultural experiment station
in Lancetilla valley*

DOROTHY POPENOE, AS I SAY, GAVE UP HER
own work in botany, but was, of course, continu-
ously interested in Pop's—in his new job, which
included all research connected with banana-growing and the creation of an experiment station in
the jungle-valley of Lancetilla, three miles from
Tela.

The United Fruit's main business—scattered
through most of Central America as well as north-

ern South America, Jamaica, and Cuba—was (still is) bananas, but the company was looking ahead to possible development of other fruits and agricultural products. Directly and, of course, primarily, Pop was working for the immediate, no less than the long-range, advantage of the firm that employed him, but he was also greatly and consistently concerned for the economic future of Latin America which—as he put it in a pamphlet written some time later—depended "largely upon the rational development of its latent agricultural resources." By this he did not mean the "exploitation of standing forests or the harvesting of crops which have been produced by unassisted nature," but, rather, "the intelligent cultivation of crop plants suited to local climatic and economic conditions. . . ."

"The crying need of diversification," he continued in that pamphlet, "is recognized by every one familiar with conditions in tropical America. No country whose prosperity depends upon a single crop—even upon two or three crops—can afford to rest content. The only solid agricultural prosperity is one built upon diversification. Not alone should there be numerous crops for export, but also food products adequate to make the country independent and self-supporting.

". . . Assuming that plant introduction has been given the attention it deserves, the next step is to investigate cultural practices, and make sure that they are adequate, not only to insure profitable crops in the immediate future, but also to permit continued utilization of the land. This phase of the problem opens up a whole field of possibilities: the best methods of propagation; the maintenance of soil fertility; crop rotation or the substitution of new crops when the land, through the invasion of specialized plant diseases, or for other reasons, is no longer adapted to the old ones; and a host of other features."

At Lancetilla, Pop covered this field of possibilities by bringing under cultivation some eighty acres of cleared jungle land. This area included twenty acres of nurseries and a great arboretum. There were rows of young citrus, avocado, tung-oil, chicle, cinnamon, and mangosteen trees; and sections devoted to rubber, and such timber trees as mahogany, teak, and Spanish cedar.

The station had the best meteorological and other necessary equipment.

As for personnel, it was, to quote Pop again, "a particular policy of the institution to receive young Latin Americans as student assistants, with a view to training them in modern methods of horticulture and agriculture."

One of these student assistants was Jorge Benitez, a young Ecuadorian of fine mind and character, whom Pop had met in the Andes and used as guide and companion while traveling for the United States Government in 1919 and 1920. Roughing it together, they had become close friends. So now, five years later, Pop sent for Jorge, who came eagerly and, although originally trained to be a carpenter and builder, he soon became a skilled plantsman—and an important factor in the lives of the Popenoes: for the friendship between Pop and Jorge presently included Dorothy.

The wet hot coastal regions of Central America

[175]

are severe on white women, especially on those of Anglo-Saxon stock. On getting there, not a few of them incline to inactivity, which gradually leads to physical and mental indolence, stagnation, carelessness with dress, a formless discontent, and a mean disposition.

Dorothy Popenoe, however, or Mrs. Pop, as the American colony in Tela began to call her, went in the other direction—with a vengeance. Within a few months she had a capable command of Spanish and had read extensively on Central American history and geography. And it was not long before she was deep in archæology.

Dorothy Popenoe digs for ruins and graves

WHILE AVOCADO-HUNTING IN GUATEMALA, Mexico, and the Andes, Wilson Popenoe had frequently come upon ancient Maya, Aztec, and Inca idols, vases, and tools, which interested him; but he inclined more to ethnology than archæology. He had come close to many of the Indian tribes of Central and South America, and for some of them he developed a profound regard. They were the real Americans, and—like Samuel Zemurray—Pop

thought they had "something." Their background
on this continent was a matter of ten or fifteen
thousand years (nobody knew how long) as
against, say, the Spaniards' or New Englanders' or
Virginians' ten or fifteen generations.

"Why," Pop would remark to Dorothy, "we're
just a bunch of greenhorns—interlopers, that's
what we are—all of us so-called whites."

Not far from Tela were the famous Copan
Ruins, and a little farther away, across the border
in the Republic of Guatemala, the Quirigua
Ruins—both startlingly vivid hints of the greatness of the old Maya civilization.

And, with all this so close around her, a person
as alive as Dorothy Popenoe could not fail to re-
spond to the call of archæology, which is probably
one of the most exciting, satisfying, and basically
important of sciences.

Besides, during the first year at Lancetilla seldom a week passed that laborers laying out the
nursery did not come upon some interesting artifacts. Bits of obsidian—flakes and broken knives
—were so common that little attention was paid to

them. The same was true of potsherds and other minor objects that turned up with every other shovelful of dirt. But Jorge Benitez, Pop's new assistant, was alert for beautifully shaped metates, or mealing stones, and various objects made of jade; for clay and polychrome figures and incense burners, and for painted pottery that had been used by the primitive pre-Columbian inhabitants of the Valley of Lancetilla.

Traveling from one banana plantation to another, Pop was often away from home for days and weeks at a time, while Dorothy occupied herself— during their first year in the tropics—with repairing and studying these unearthed objects, and making notes on them that were ultimately incorporated in a pamphlet on the findings in Lancetilla which she wrote in collaboration with Pop.

In archæology, as in most other fields of study or endeavor, one thing leads to another.

In July 1927, after securing the permission of the Honduran Government and the financial support of an American foundation, Dorothy Popenoe—accompanied by Jorge Benitez—began the exploring, mapping, and photographing of the pre-Columbian ruins of Tenampua, located on a mountain-top near Comayagua, in Honduras. In a few weeks she completed the job, then wrote a paper which was published by the Honduran Government in Spanish and by the Smithsonian Institution in English.

Some one has said that all true archæologists are ghouls; so next we find Dorothy following a rumor that somewhere along the river Ulua, also in Honduras, was an ancient cemetery with graves containing important and interesting articles of pottery and other artifacts that had been interred with the bodies. She found the place, organized a digging party, and unearthed, along with skeletons, a vast lot of glorious junk.

At this digging, she did more work than most of the men in her party. Jorge, her loyal and able aid, had to warn her repeatedly not to overwork herself.

The Restoration

The digging completed, she wrote a paper which was published by the Middle American Research Department of Tulane University of Louisiana. I cannot refrain from quoting from it characteristic passages:

In February 1928, while I was engaged in an investigation of some ruins on a hill near Pimienta, one of my workmen mentioned Playa de los Muertos as a place where pottery and bones were frequently found. I had long wanted to visit this site where Byron Gordon [well-known archæologist of a previous generation] had worked, but had hitherto been uncertain as to its exact location. Upon ascertaining that my informant knew the place well, I secured him as a guide, and with two others of my men rode across the country from Pimienta. Traversing lands belonging to the Cayumel Fruit Company, we arrived finally at Santiago.

In a small headland about 100 meters upstream from Santiago and two meters from the top of the bank, a flat shelf three meters wide had been washed out; it was covered with fragments of bone and pottery, suggesting that burials had originally been located at this level. Leaving the shelf behind we pursued the line of this stratum upstream, and a few meters distant discovered two graves lying one meter apart. We opened both hastily and found the bodies, unflexed, with the heads face downward, directed toward the river.

As this part of the land was well above water, the

hot sun had baked it very hard, making it impossible, in the limited time at our disposal, to secure even the heads intact.

The first burial was evidently that of a young person. The bones were slight, and the wisdom teeth still embedded within the jawbones. On the left wrist was a bracelet of tiny perforated shells.

The skeleton in the second grave was larger, with the teeth much ground down. The head had been crushed flat by the weight of earth that had lain over it. On the left side, near the feet, were two fair sized monochrome pots, one inverted over the other. There was also a pair of flat black stones with cutting edges that may have served as chopping tools.

We then took the cayuco and made an examination of the lowest section of the bank. A little below the water and over five meters from the top we came upon a skull partly exposed by the washing of the river. The earth here was soft, and it was an easy matter to remove the head intact. It was exceedingly regrettable that a short while later my cayuquero should unwittingly have allowed it to fall into the stream. A cloud of mud rising to the boat was the last I saw of my prize. At the base of the neck were a number of jadeite beads and three small polished pendants of the same material worked in the form of hatchets.

The hours had passed too rapidly and the light was already failing. Reluctantly I set out again for my camp in the forest. I had seen enough, however, to realize that the site merited investigation, and I decided that if it were possible I would return after the following flood season was over. . . .

The winter rains of 1928 held off so long that I planned to make some excavations at Playa de los Muertos before the river should begin to rise. Accordingly, on November 5th of that year, I arrived at the site, accompanied by four men and a well furnished outfit.

We were too late. The same day the perverse river rose five feet, and by nightfall had completely inundated the place where I wanted to work. There was no alternative but to return to Tela and await the advent of the dry season.

Three months later the rains had ceased and the river had subsided almost to its minimum level.

With an outfit consisting of five men who camped on the site to guard it night and day, and instruments for excavating, mapping and photography, I tried my luck again. All seemed to be in our favor. The ground was soft from the recent rains, while the cloudless sky promised fair weather for our work.

The winter floods had altered the topography of the site considerably. The shelf of the year before had been washed out many feet inland and down to within one meter of the water's edge. Where the local inhabitants had been picking over the ground with machetes in the hope of finding artifacts, scattered shreds were abundant, though skeletal remains were lacking.

[183]

The House in Antigua

Our first procedure was to examine closely the whole of the bank against which the downstream current was driving. The upper burial stratum in which we found two skeletons the previous year had been completely washed out. But at a certain point over five meters from the top of the bank, a white patch, seemingly the top of a cranium, was gleaming through the water.

This was the starting point of our excavations which were commenced by slicing away the bank from the top to the water's edge in a strip two meters wide by three meters long. I then lay on the ledge thus formed, and with the precaution of a rope around my waist, removed the soil, little by little, from around the skull. It lay face downwards, and all of it was badly cracked, not from the force of the current, I believe, but from the tremendous weight of earth previously superimposed upon it. I removed the pieces, and was later able to reconstruct it almost entirely. Thirteen bright green jadeite beads glinted through the water in the region of the neck. It is more than likely that a number had already been washed away by the stream.

While searching for scapulae and vertebrae a small brown pottery dish was found, placed where the right shoulder should have been. For almost a meter inland no further trace of bones appeared until I struck the base of a pelvis. Subsequent excavation revealed that this did not belong to the owner of the skull but to another

[184]

body lying apparently in the same grave but oriented in the opposite direction.

Burial No. 2

The position of this skeleton on the right side with arms flexed so that the hands came beneath the face, and legs doubled straight back from the pelvis. The head was completely crushed in laterally and all the bones excessively soft owing to the fact that it was partly submerged at the time of excavation. The use of any kind of tool was out of the question. Most of the cleaning was accomplished by repeatedly pouring small panfuls of water over the bones.

Adhering with earth to the maxilla was a fine jadeite ornament, three centimeters long. Another, similar in shape, but smaller and of a much finer stone, the color equal to that of high grade oriental jade, was found underneath the face. They had probably served as finger ornaments, but the poor condition of the bones prevented my being able to verify this. A round bowl of a pleasing blue grey color stood close to the back of the head.

On two occasions, during the excavations of these burials, I had reason to be thankful for the safety rope attached to me. The swift current took little time in undermining our sodden shelf of land. A crack would appear; then without further warning a thick vertical slab would slide into the water. The second time that my shelf dissolved away beneath me, however, it disclosed another head directed toward the river (SW 195°), less than a meter downstream from the first grave.

[185]

The House in Antigua

Burial No. 3

. . . The skeleton in this grave . . . was completely
unflexed, and laid face downwards. The arms were close
to the sides of the body, and flexed at the elbows, so that
the hands lay beneath the face.

The head was raised intact after having been left to
dry for a week. The fact that it had suffered somewhat
from pressure may or may not be sufficient to account
for its appearance of artificial flattening such as was a
common practice among the early Mayas.

Burial No. 4

While I was occupied in opening graves Nos. 1, 2 and
3, the workmen were engaged in stripping away that
part of the bank, a few meters downstream, where I had
found two burial strata the previous year. No trace of
the upper stratum was left. The lower one in the same
vicinity yielded eleven graves in all and a large variety
of objects.

Burial No. 4 had evidently been discovered before our
arrival by local treasure seekers. The entire skeleton as
far as the knees had been thrown away. At this point the
work had ceased, for the bank rose steeply and was not
easy to dig out. Doubtless, too, the task had proved un-
profitable. A little more perseverance would have disclosed the fact that all the artifacts belonging to it were
deposited at the feet. We encountered no less than twelve
objects neatly stacked on either side.

. . . . .

The Restoration

Burial No. 7

Shortly before my arrival at Playa de los Muertos the occupant of grave No. 7 became the victim of local curiosity and the prevalent fear of "muertos." The probing blade of a machete struck his head. His narrow bed was then opened in search of hidden treasure, apparently without success. Hope being disappointed, fear must have crept in, for his head having been taken out, was hastily reinterred much the worse for wear, with the mandible inverted.

This, at least, is my interpretation of the story of one of my visitors, who related to me how she had taken up a complete skeleton and buried it again without harming a bone of it. I did not find it worth while to ask what she had done with the trunk which was entirely wanting.

While cleaning the dirt from the back of the head, I found what she had evidently missed—a little jadeite amulet pierced for suspension. A few centimeters from the right knee were two tiny pots that contained a paint-like substance, and a smooth slightly concave stone that may have been used for preparing it. There were also three obsidian knives. . . .

Burial No. 8

It was impossible to banish sentiment while working on this little grave. Within was the skeleton of a small child whose delicate skull had been crushed flat from the weight of the earth. Most of the milk teeth were in place, although one or two were missing from the upper jaw.

The face was turned upwards, and the legs, folded straight back from the pelvis, lay close beside the arms.

The character of the rich assortment of jewels and artifacts seemed peculiarly appropriate to their possessor. Around the throat was a necklace of white shell beads relieved by a central pendant of carved shell and two minute lateral pendants of worked jadeite. A double row of jadeite beads encompassed the waist. As the whole body was raised intact, together with the earth in which it was embedded, only the loose beads from the surface were removed. These numbered ninety-three; doubtless more will be found when the bones are lifted.

A drinking vessel of thin pale clay stood upon the head, while the chest supported three dishes of good workmanship. Two clay figurines, or dolls, one eleven, the other only six centimeters long, protruded from beneath the finest of the vessels. The latter was composed of two chambers, one crowned by a human head and the other surmounted by a hollow loop in the center of which was the opening to the vessel.

Conclusion

The work of which this paper is a brief description must be considered only as another scratch upon the surface of vast archæological deposits in the Ulua Valley.

Every piece of research that has been accomplished in this region seems to have served rather to produce new problems than to solve old ones. And this will continue, no doubt, until wide and diligent search has revealed most of the secrets hidden by the ancient river.

The Restoration

Perhaps one of the most striking problems is the riddle of the different types of pottery. At certain points in the river—for example Playa de los Muertos, described in this report—all the pottery found in both upper and lower strata is of the simple monochrome type, while at Rancheria, about eight kilometers upstream on the same side, a rich dump of polychrome ware yielded fragments as beautiful as some of the finest Central 'American examples. Time and moisture had failed to dim the brilliancy of the colors.

Similar fragments have been encountered inland during the opening of ditches and irrigation canals. It seems inconceivable that these two distinct types of ware could have been manufactured by the same people, and equally strange, that tribes differing widely in cultural traits could have been living synchronously in such close proximity.

In the burials examined at Playa de los Muertos, the artifacts from the two strata have been of the same type. But it is noticeable that no jadeite was found in the two graves of the upper stratum, while the lower burial layers yielded a considerable number of amulets and beads of fine quality jadeite.

Signs of human occupation were visible throughout the bank at this point. Wood ashes, charcoal and unbaked clay were frequently encountered; shells were abundant, particularly at one spot where a shell-heap was excavated. Here were sufficient shells, all of the same species, to fill three large meal sacks. . . .

It would be difficult to gauge with any degree of accuracy the length of time that was necessary for the river to lay down five meters of alluvium over these graves. The Ulua changes its course from year to year, depositing at one point what it steals from another. A hint as to the rapidity of this process may be gained from a study of the little island immediately below the headland in which excavations were conducted. According to local "oldest inhabitants," seven years ago it was not in existence. Since that time the river has built it up to the present height of about three meters.

The time will come, it is to be hoped, when conjecture on the past history of the Ulua will pass into fact. But the information whereby this will be attained still lies hidden in the field awaiting future investigation.

I quote from this archæological report at such length because, although it was meant to be (and is) objective and scientific, it tells much about her work and is also an effective piece of unconscious, indirect verbal autoportraiture.

It reveals her mind as unhurried, uncluttered. Her logical sentences proceed patiently, with unstudied simplicity, and stick close to the subject. There is no superfluous phrase or word; no striving for effect. Her information is precise, her expression clear. She was meticulous, economical, exact.

The Restoration

Dorothy had a keen, finely subdued sense of humor. "I did not find it worth while to ask what she had done with the trunk (of the corpse) which was entirely wanting."

She was calm, well-controlled; had not been irrationally aroused by the damage done to the skeletons by the local ghouls and bungling amateur diggers who had opened the burials before she came there. She was grateful for what she got, uncomplainingly accepted the situation, and painstakingly sifted the disturbed scene for possibilities.

She obviously wanted to be considered solely on the merit of her work, with no deference to the fact that she was a woman. Observe the almost apologetic note in the description of Burial No. 8, where she tells of finding the skeleton of a baby. She signed the paper "*D. H.* Popenoe."

She writes a diary and adds to her
self-portrait

I N SLIGHTLY MORE THAN NINE YEARS OF HER
married life Dorothy Popenoe bore five children,
and took care of them.

At the same time, she read voluminously, traveled professionally and for pleasure, corresponded
with dozens of people in the United States, England, Guatemala, and elsewhere; trained herself
to draw so that she was able to illustrate her archæological reports with authentic pen-and-ink

sketches; studied French and German because much of the scientific literature that interested her was in those languages; followed current events; experimented with writing; kept a file on the various things that drew her attention; filled several loose-leaf notebooks with all sorts of data and personal reflections; and late in 1929—before she, Wilson Popenoe, and their children left Honduras for Guatemala—began a diary of which even her husband was unaware while she lived.

How she managed to do all this is more than anyone with whom I talked about her, including Pop, can explain. Most of my informants simply described her as "tireless," "marvelously able." Yet her diary contains frequent self-reproaches— she was never doing and accomplishing enough.

To all who came in contact with her she appeared an unusually happy, well-functioning person. And this she doubtless was. But it seems that she was completely and uninterruptedly happy about only one thing: that Wilson Popenoe was her husband.

The central and constant fact and force of her

being was a vital necessity for development, growth, and function. She was not ambitious, but had a keen inner urgency for achievement and for order within and about her; and such people never know when they are doing enough or too much for their strength; they cannot afford to feel tired—except for a moment now and then.

This she revealed in her diary, which was written, incidentally, in a neat, clear hand in a leather-bound regulation engineer's fieldbook:

NOVEMBER 28. . . . I examine my daily life. I am not satisfied. . . . I have not enough time. Why? My life is easy. I have plenty of domestic help. Eulogio [the cook] is becoming well trained and Laura and Louise [house-maids] are above average. The fault must be with me in being a poor executive. The incessant and petty interruptions, which even the busiest executives experience, should not interrupt my main stream of thought and effort. To use Wilson's words, I must become more "hard boiled." And just because the climate is against me, I must make the greatest struggle to obtain the mental freedom that is heaven on earth. At the same time I must not forget the philosophy of relaxation. By better methods I ought to be able to find and use more spare moments than hitherto.

Resolution No. 1: Be more methodical. Running the

house needs more method than brains. Fulfill as much as possible the running of the household first thing in the morning. Treat it as a superficial care while the main mental themes run their course uninterrupted.

Resolution No. 2: Write to supplement thought and memory. This is important. I cannot write too much. Write down the menus for the day and the girl's duties. Do not teach Eulogio a new recipe without writing it down. Keep memo pads with pencils always on hand. Classify the duties in groups so that odd jobs of similar nature may be carried out at once to save time: telephone calls, gifts of vegetables to friends, etc.

Resolution No. 3: Do not give unnecessary attention to the children. Be generous in helping Nancy [her oldest daughter, then not quite four] to unfold her mind with stories and work. Keep a list of things for her to do on wet days and fine. . . . Do not superintend, or interfere too frequently in, the children's play. They need to be left alone and play by themselves. See that Nancy has plenty of companions, then forget her.

Resolution No. 4: Never cook a dish when raw foods are as good, or when Eulogio can cook instead.

Resolution No. 5: Seek solitude for work and meditation whenever possible. This saves energy and helps to maintain order in the house. Keep the guest-room and desk as sacred for work. Spend at least one to two hours there daily. Keep material on the desk arranged methodically to encourage tidiness of thought. Make ample notes and file them away. Pencils and pens should be at every desk to save time hunting for them. . . . Make a habit of thinking while engaged in manual work. My mind is lazy and my fingers active. Don't let the fingers be an excuse for the mind to sleep. . . . Read only good books.

NOVEMBER 29.—Today has been most satisfactory. With my thoughts better clarified, I do actually seem to have more time. . . . Cleaned and arranged guest-room closet. Taught Eulogio and wrote out for him recipe for gypsy stew. . . . Reconstructed some pottery [from the Ulua River graves] with plaster. Called on Mrs. M. and returned Dimnet's *Art of Thinking*. . . . I played a little tennis but was too tired to play much. Cleaned out Wilson's two drawers—socks and handkerchiefs. . . .

A most interesting letter came from a girl, Margaret Michel, in Havana, Cuba. She is Swiss and a friend of the German girl, Miss Wunderlich, whom Wilson met some months ago. She is applying for post of governess and has diploma for teaching French, English, German, and music. I cannot help feeling excited over it. I do not know how much she would require in wages. Too much, I fear. But if she were a nice girl, how fine it would be to have her! She could teach me French and German and Nancy kindergarten and Spanish. But the greatest of all would be to be able to accompany Wilson whenever he wanted me. I could do without lots of things in order to be by his side and not tied down to the babies. And the archæology too! It is a delightful dream, if nothing else. I will write to Wilson about it now. . . .

Weighed myself today: 118 lb. It is a little too much but satisfactory, for I am still nursing Hugh, and two months back weighed 125. Hugh began to smile at five weeks of age. Today (he is three months) he laughed out loud when I played peek-a-boo with him. . . . Nancy ran into my room (she always runs instead of walks) asking to have [her friends] John Rollins and his sister to supper: I said no, because Laura was not here to get it. "Very well," said Nancy, "then I will get it myself," and forthwith dragged out the little table and chairs, laid cloth, napkins, and spoons; got glasses of water, ran into the garden and cut a pretty bouquet of flowers. The only thing she had to ask for was a vase to put them in, and in less than ten minutes, when her guests arrived, everything was in readiness. That is quick and well-ordered thinking. . . . I now read to her out of books instead of telling her stories. Tonight I read her Cinderella. . . . Wrote to Wilson.

NOVEMBER 30.—Mailed two letters to Wilson, New Orleans. . . . Continued reconstructing of pottery with plaster of Paris. I need more wax and the tiny plane to make a good job of it. . . . Cleaned the two drawers in my dresser. . . . Played tennis and had a swim afterward. At 8 p.m. too tired to write much.

DECEMBER 1.—Stayed in bed till 8 a.m. and was still pretty tired during the day, so played no tennis. Apparently I have gone too far, as usual. It needs a delicate adjustment to concentrate and relax at the same time. Yet that is productive of best results, a good illustration being tennis. "Eyes on the ball," that is concentration,

The House in Antigua

yet sufficient relaxation to keep a clear head. I have never forgotten how at school when I was frowning in a great effort over a piece of music I found difficult, Miss Whish said, "Play it as though it were easy." . . .

Read through three numbers of the New York *Times* Book Review with red pencil and scissors. The articles referring to subjects that interest us I cut out and placed in books of similar interest in the library. . . . Sent baskets of vegetables to Mrs. Whittaker and Mrs. Blanco. . . . Oiled and mended Nancy's motorcar which she can ride now quite well.

DECEMBER 2.—Two adorable letters from Wilson today. I believe he must be in New Orleans now and will sail from there this Friday to arrive here Wednesday. If only he were here now! . . . Nancy's prattle never ceases for a moment while she is in the house, and it is all directed at me. If I give up everything and just pay attention to her, she is happy, naturally. But if I ignore it or check her in this most natural of impulses, she becomes miserable or defiant immediately. . . . Took her to the Commissary this morning to look at the Christmas toys. Also had Dorothy Speh with me. I observe a very few toys are in any way instructive or constructive. Mostly mechanical and completely finished. Searched for something like a toolchest, without luck. Did find a washing-mangling-and-ironing set which may help to keep Nancy occupied for a while.

DECEMBER 3.—Wrote to Wilson, his last letter before

[198]

he comes! . . . Afternoon went to town and bought a few toys. Must make out a list of children and their gifts. Met George Gorman on the way back. Came in house and had a long talk. Gave him two small pieces of weaving to give his mother—he is just going home on vacation. . . .

In *The Living Age* for November, there is a translation from *L'Europe Nouvelle* containing four letters from Flaubert to Turgenev, written between 1872-78. In my ignorance I do not know who they are but seem to be writers of renown. Flaubert is about to commence writing *Herodias* and he thinks his task is not easy. "I hope to start writing in about a week. At present I am in an abominable funk and fear that I ought to have devotions said for nine days, praying for the success of my enterprise!" Surely this should encourage lesser mortals!

DECEMBER 5.—Awoke to find house in the middle of a lake of water and firewood all floating round the house. Barometer very high, raining hard, little wind. Nancy thought it all a huge joke and after breakfast got into her bathing suit and shoes. She and I were Mr. and Mrs. Noah, and she went outside in search of Mount Ararat and incidentally her motorcar, which had been left under the house. Had a great time. . . . The baby is a comical little fellow. He shouts and coughs to attract attention and is always smiling. . . . Two adorable letters from Wilson. Only five more days to wait now before he comes.

DECEMBER 6.—This month's *Atlantic* is a splendid number. . . . Worked on restoring pottery this morning but was not very successful. In two cases the plaster broke. Perhaps I should not attempt to work it in wet weather. . . . Half promised Nancy to clean and paint her car to-morrow.

DECEMBER 7.—Did paint Nancy's car. Took me nearly all morning. Looks pretty—green finished with a black stripe, black enamel "works," and yellow wheels.

DECEMBER 8.— . . . Have been getting blue lately, but this will all go after Wilson gets back.

At this time Dorothy developed a great interest in meteorology, especially in the study of the unpleasant damp north wind that during the winter months frequently blew over the northeast coast of Honduras. She observed the thermometer, kept careful note of the readings, and worked out a method of predicting when a norther would come. Every other day or so she recorded something about this in the diary. On December third, for instance, she wrote; "Barometer rising to high this morning. Called Bob Beasley (in the United Fruit manager's office) and predicted

norther within next twenty-four hours, this
afternoon or to-morrow morning. It came this
afternoon."

When Pop returned home, she was writing an
article on her method of predicting the norther.
When she finished it (to quote again from the
diary) ,

he corrected it and had it copied, but advises against
publishing it. He feels there is room for criticism of the
spirit of it—that I am announcing the accuracy of my
prophecy. So I am not sending it. He knows so much
better than I do, that I accept his advice wholeheartedly.
Nevertheless, I must be honest in my own mind. I do
not agree with him. It seems to me harmless and interesting. . . . We are now in the midst of another norther,
which I am noting down as before, with this addition—
am making wind maps from day to day of data gathered
on radio reports. I am not sure if Wilson cares for me to
do all this. He either feels I am plunging in where angels
fear to tread, and making bold assumptions on very
slender data and observations at only one station; or he
feels meteorology is more his subject than mine, and that
the work should be done rather from the Lancetilla station where they are well equipped, and through official
sources, rather than down here, with nothing but a
barometer! He says little about it, so will refrain from
questioning him—just watch him.

The House in Antigua

Two days later:

I was all wrong about Wilson's idea. He is quite satisfied to have me try to hold up meteorology at this end. Last week's norther came out exactly as predicted and it is apparent that Mr. R. [manager of the fruit company] is quite keen about it. Wilson and I have even discussed the possibility of a station here with rain gauge and other instruments.

Further quotations from the diary:

DECEMBER 19.— . . . It is wonderful to have Wilson back again. The little dinners and evenings together are so satisfying. . . . He and I are both reading Remarque's *All Quiet on the Western Front*; it is a terrific book. . . . Feeling depressed again. No idea why. Seems so silly when I have all in the world I could wish for. . . .

JANUARY 4.—Wilson left early yesterday morning in airplane for Castilla. He then goes to Jamaica. We were both very disconsolate about his having to leave again so soon. Mr. Rowe wants him in Jamaica to find out what is the matter with the bananas there. It is splendid he is so much in demand and I must not be so selfish about it. I had even planned to accompany him as far as Cuba, but that was frustrated by his going in the plane.

JANUARY 5.—Gibsons came to dinner last night. Dinner was not very good as it was spoiled by being kept too long, the guests arriving late. . . . Weighed Hugh last

The Restoration

Wednesday, January 1st. He is 15 lbs. and about 2 ounces. I am 113, Nancy 35. . . . Hugh is now almost weaned. I have just begun on only one nursing in the early morning. I am trying to teach him to drink out of a cup by giving him his orange juice that way, but he does not like it. . . .

JANUARY 7.—Yesterday was a great day. Received radiogram from Wilson saying he would arrive in Tela in the evening on the *Turrialba* and would stay a few hours only. At five o'clock the boat was sighted and I went down to meet it. Owing to a strong current she did not dock till nearly seven. . . . I went on board to precious Wilson. Had a cocktail with Mr. Rollins and dinner with Wilson afterward. He then came home for about an hour. Of course Hugh chose to kick up a fuss and Nancy wanted a story and I lost patience. However, they quieted down and I had an hour of peace with Wilson. . . . Tonight the Butlers came to dinner.

JANUARY 15.—Mail today. . . . Mrs. Whitehouse is sending a package for Hugh. It is bound to be something nice. . . .

A surprising occurrence. Nancy came in at 11 a.m. from playing outside and rushed to me smiling with outstretched arms and laid her head in my lap. Suddenly she caught hold of my sleeve in her teeth and bit right into the flesh of my arm as hard as she could. I said, very surprised, "Why, Nancy, do you know you are hurting me?" She was silent a moment and then said, "Yes, be-

[203]

cause you did not give me what I wanted last night."
(This was not true. She had been quite content the
previous evening.) I did not reprimand her, but turned
back to my desk where I was sitting and continued my
letter-writing. She went away crying and cried for some
time. Luncheon bell rang. I washed my hands without
inviting her. Laura told her to come to the table, but she
said No. I took my soup alone, reading a book. I could
hear that she was trying to defend her ego by shutting
herself in her room and there singing loudly. As I still
continued to read, she opened the door and said, "I was
not singing for you, I was singing for myself." Still no
notice. Soon after, when she saw hot biscuits coming, she
came to me and said she was sorry. I was puzzled by the
whole proceeding. She was happy when she came to me,
yet suddenly bit me. It seemed unnatural for a little
child like that to harbor a grievance and take revenge
with no sign of anger or sulkiness. It then dawned on me
suddenly that it was probably a little touch of sadism, a
glint of primitiveness, that surprised her as much as it
did me. She hurt me because she loved me (?) and all
the subsequent behavior was merely an attempt at ration-
alization.

This is not an "intimate" journal; it reveals no
Dostoevskian depths of Dorothy's character, no
muddy swirls in the flow of her life. Yet the diary
is probably as intimate as it could be. Dorothy
Popenoe was not a complex person; one of her

steadiest tendencies was toward simplicity and still more simplicity.

She was exquisitely feminine, but her diary contains very few references to clothes. Only now and then she noted: "I sent for two dresses," or some such bare fact. She had solved her dress problem in a way that was typical of her. Soon after her marriage she had discovered, and Pop agreed with her, that a certain simple kind of Czech "peasant" dress became her better than anything else; and so that was all she wore the rest of her life. When one group of these dresses wore out, she ordered another, or Pop bought them for her when he happened to go to the States. Occasionally one of them needed altering, which she did herself. This was the simplest way of keeping herself in clothes, least expensive of time, effort, and money.

The Popenoes move to the
Guatemalan highlands

W ITH THE UNITED STATES AS ITS CHIEF MARKET, the banana business was at its height in the final years of Coolidge Prosperity; and early in 1929, holding with the "best minds" in America that good times were certain to continue under Hoover, the United Fruit Company decided upon a program of expansion in Guatemala. A large tract of dank jungle country beneath the volcanoes on the west coast was to be cleared and its prodigious fertility turned to producing bananas.

[206]

The Restoration

Even before this decision was made, Wilson Popenoe had spent a good deal of time on the west coast of Guatemala, studying the soil, rainfall and other climatic conditions, and taking charge of the general investigational work looking toward the development of the proper technique of banana-growing in that region.

Then—early in 1930, while every one was reassuring every one else that the Crash of the previous autumn was nothing to disturb one's head about—the Company suggested to him that, since during the next four years he would be required to devote most of his time and energy to the new development, he should move his office and his family from Tela to Guatemala City.

Both Pop and Dorothy, who had made several brief visits with him to the Guatemalan highlands before this, greeted the suggestion with joy.

One reason for this was that now, in Guatemala, Pop would be able to put into effect an idea he had been working on for some time. This was the so-called Servicio Tecnico de Cooperación Agricola. The United Fruit Company and the International Railways of Central America, also foreign-owned, had agreed to sponsor jointly the development of a number of small experiment stations in the different climatic zones of Guatemala, where Pop and his assistants would introduce and experiment with new crop plants of promise; the results to be for the benefit of the Guatemalan agriculturists. The companies' motive in this was largely political: to improve the country's feeling toward them. And, as an employee of the United Fruit, Pop was interested in that too; but, as at Lancetilla, he was also eager to tap the country's latent agricultural possibilities.

The Popenoes moved to Guatemala City at once and rented a house on the outskirts of the town, near the residences of some other American families.

The Servicio Tecnico de Cooperación Agricola was very close to Pop's heart, and he threw himself into the project, which forthwith evoked much interest throughout Guatemala. People everywhere offered him land on which to establish small experiment stations, and he started them at Antigua, Capetillo, Tecpán, and Lake Atitlan. The technical staff of the United Fruit were the Servicio's consulting experts on soils, insect pests, and plant diseases; meteorologists, and others. They introduced promising new fruits and other plants, propagated and gave them to farmers, and wrote instructive articles for local publications. The project was a cross between an experiment station and an agricultural extension service.

This, along with the investigational work in the future banana jungles on the west coast, took Pop away much of the time, but he spent weekends at home almost regularly, and occasionally he was required to work a whole week at the office in Guatemala City: which was the most attractive feature of the Popenoes' new circumstances. In Honduras, they had been fortunate if they spent together three, four days a month.

But now, in Guatemala, Dorothy was happy about many other things. This climate was so fine for the children. There was a good German kindergarten school. The shops in the city offered so much more than had been obtainable at the Com-

pany commissary in Tela. There were private col-
lections of rare volumes on archæology and the
history of Middle America from which she could
borrow.

She had had friends at Tela, but none had
shared her interest in archæology and the history
of Central America; while here in Guatemala
City was the Honduras-Guatemala-El Salvador
headquarters of the Carnegie Institution. The city
was a center of activity also for Frans Blom and
others of the Middle America Research. Mr. and
Mrs. Oliver Ricketson, of the Institution, had a
house near hers and became her friends, as did
Sheldon and Mary Alexander Whitehouse, the
American Minister and his wife, whose home—
the Legation—also was not far away.

Another virtue of Guatemala City in the Popenoes' eyes was its proximity to Antigua. They
owned a Ford, and they drove there as often as
time permitted them: about once a month. The
trip took only a little over an hour.

They wandered through the ruins, visited Pop's

The Restoration

friends and acquaintances from his avocado-exploration days and had unfailingly a happy time. The fascination and strange charm of Antigua seized Dorothy as they had seized Pop years previously . . . and it was not long before they decided to buy the ruin popularly known as the Casa del Capuchino, and to restore it.

The restoration of Casa del Capuchino begins

NOT A FEW OF THE POPENOES' FRIENDS THOUGHT them mad, and some did not hesitate to tell them so. The ruin looked a hopeless mess: how *could* one "restore" it? True, some of the walls remained, but all were cracked: and how was that main corner going to be put back into plumb? The cypress in the middle of the main patio, they all agreed, was indeed a wonderful tree; one could hardly take one's eyes from it; but the patio, like the smaller inner courts in the rear, was nothing

[212]

more than a dump-heap. The poor people living in the place during the past century and a half had first shoveled into it all the dirt and débris from the rooms, and had then continued to throw on top of that the refuse of their meager daily living. How, the Popenoes' friends asked, were they even going to clean up the place? And why should anyone *want* to "restore" it? . . .

Dorothy smiled at this well-meaning talk and Pop enjoyed it, too. It continued for months after the American and English colonies in Guatemala City and the United Fruit people down in the jungles learned of their purchasing the ruin.

Antigua, of course, was agog. The Señor Doctor and Señora Popenoe had bought the Casa del Capuchino and would rebuild it as it had been originally, three hundred years ago. What do you think of that? was the question everybody was asking everybody else. How long would it take to restore it? And, once restored, was it going to be a museum or a private home? . . .

The Popenoes' intention, which they kept more or less to themselves, was to rebuild the

house carefully, little by little. It might take anywhere from five to ten years. They did not know
how soon Pop's job might return them to Honduras, or take them to Costa Rica, Colombia, or
some other place where the United Fruit had extensive plantations. They did not permit themselves to dream of living in Antigua for any length
of time during the next ten or fifteen years. But
they planned to come here, or Dorothy alone,
every once in a while to work on the restoration.
Then—eventually, after Pop retired and the children were grown or away in school or college—
they would settle in the restored house and write
books and read . . . make trips further into these
highlands . . . dig for Mayan ruins and pottery,
and study Guatemalan Indians, and plant life.

This was their dream.

Immediately after they bought the ruin, Pop
and Dorothy faced an interesting human situation.
Most of the tenants living in the place were as
poor as they could possibly be. The ninety-foot-

long sala was partitioned into four "rooms," each occupied by a family, a couple, or an individual.

One of the tenants in the sala was an aged widow without relatives or income, Señora Teresa Mairen, who kept body and soul together on less than a dollar a month, which she procured begging. She had been living in the Casa del Capuchino for twenty-odd years. No, she had paid no rent either to Señora Ruiz or to Señor Peralta, the last two owners prior to the Popenoes; they had generously allowed her to stay rent-free and, in return for their beneficence, she had prayed for them twice daily before the tomb of Hermano Pedro. Now, if they (the Popenoes) asked her to leave, which they had a right to ask her—where could she go?

Pop and Dorothy planned to begin the restoration in the rear patios and systematically work toward the front, and they figured it would take them two or three years to get anywhere near the sala; so they told the old woman to stay until then. When it became necessary for her to vacate, they would "pension" her, so she could live elsewhere.

The House in Antigua

(The restoration of the sala was begun late in
1932; Señora Mairen was "pensioned" and received a small sum monthly till her death of old
age early in 1936.)

Another of these "rooms" in the sala was occupied by a man who earned a meager livelihood
as a clerk in the local post-office. He had been paying fifty cents rent a month. Unwilling to be land-
lords, the Popenoes would not accept the rental;
a proud man, he moved.

The two other parties living in the sala "rooms"
moved when the Popenoes acquired the house—
possibly for the same reason. They offered no explanation.

Among those living in other parts of the Casa
del Capuchino was a part-Indian woman named
Maria Garcia, in her early forties, recently wid-
owed, and mother of three daughters: Julia, who
was eleven; Victoria, ten, and Conchita, five.
Maria's husband had been a bit overfond of drink,
none too industrious, nor very foresighted, and
had left her and the children in low circumstances.
When Dorothy and Wilson Popenoe appeared,

she asked them if they could not use her and the
girls: for they all loved the cypress tree and wanted
very much to stay in the Casa del Capuchino and
do what they could to aid the Señor Doctor and
Señora Dorotea in restoring it. Both Dorothy and
Pop liked the woman, and they engaged her as a
sort of woman-about-the-place, which position
gradually evolved into that of housekeeper.

Another tenant was Arturo Santis, master-
mason, who had a family and was none too well-
off; for work in Antigua was very irregular. The
Popenoes gave him a job and—working steadily
for more than six years, with two or three helpers
—he did all the mason work necessary in the restoration, and earned the appellation "Maestro."

The same happened with still another resident
of the ruined house—Julio Gomez, a woodworker,
who was engaged to do what he could for the
restoration of the house with his trade.

In short, Dorothy and Wilson Popenoe found
on the spot a major part of the talent and labor
power needed for the reconstruction.

Invaluable to the project was their friend and

assistant, Jorge Benitez, who, as already told, had
been trained to be a carpenter and builder in his
native Ecuador. Some time before the Popenoes'
purchase of the ruin he became the manager of
the Servicio Tecnico station in Antigua, married
a charming Antigueña, and in his spare time—
while Dorothy Popenoe still lived and later, till
the job was completed—supervised the practical
details of the work of Arturo Santis, Julio Gomez,
and the other workmen.

Dorothy and Pop discussed many of the details
of the restoration and drew some of the plans for
it together, but he insists that he deserves little, if
any, credit for it. This is partly to be ascribed to
his modesty; but it is also true that the spade work,
which was the basis for the general quality the
Casa del Capuchino ultimately attained under the
hands of the workmen and the supervisory eyes of
Jorge, was done by Dorothy.

Her approach and attitude to the task of re-
creating the house out of the wreckage were essentially the same as those which had made her a

successful botanist and archæologist, wife and
mother, amateur meteorologist, writer, and pen-
and-ink artist. The mood she took to it was the
mood she brought to nearly every other enterprise
or problem. The idea was simple: to evoke order
out of a mess. It appealed to her profoundly. She
devised a method, a system, a plan; then pro-
ceeded to carry it out, simply, directly, efficiently,
patiently.

One hundred and twenty-five cartfuls of muck
and litter were hauled out of the main patio alone
—but this only after every load had been carefully
sifted either by herself personally or by a responsible workman who had instructions to put aside
every stone or roof- or floor-tile that could be used
again, as well as every bit of metal-, wood-, or
stone-work the muckers might come upon. With
this painstaking care and patience, she and the
men found in those dump-heaps, which disasters,
Time, and ill-organized humanity had piled up,
all manner of broken things that suggested to her
how certain sections of the house and some of its
furnishings had looked before the earthquakes.

[219]

Here they came upon a part of a door panel: enough to enable her to sketch a design which then made it possible for Julio Gomez, the woodworker, to re-create a seventeenth-century Spanish Renaissance door. Here was a round, thin piece of wood badly rotted, but the carving on it still sufficiently clear to tell her how the original window-grilles had looked.

Here was a part of a carved bedpost—ample basis for an imaginative reconstruction of the entire bed. Here was an old, badly rusted lock; a door bolt; a hinge from a window shutter; and so on—all very valuable to her constructive mind.

The ground in one of the patios, where several coffee trees grew, seemed too high to her. She took a shovel and, digging awhile, discovered the interesting masonry-bordered flowerbeds.

She went about the town, sometimes alone, sometimes with Wilson or Jorge, and she found and bought such things as the fountain now in the main patio, facing the entranceway; several benches, chests and coffers, tables, chairs, and doors which no one esteemed particularly, but whose origin she could trace to the pre-earthquake era.

Where new materials were required, she used only the best. Thus, for instance, she ordered lumber for the beams and ceilings from the great cypress forest in the Chichoy Mountains, ten thousand feet above sea level, above the town of Tecpán, some twenty miles from Antigua, where cypress wood is especially durable, capable of lasting for many centuries.

Most of the bricks in the sala floor were broken or worn deep in spots by many feet; but that brand of brick was no longer made anywhere in Guatemala, so Dorothy prepared the molds to reproduce them especially for the job.

Arturo Santis the mason, Julio Gomez the woodworker, and all the other skilled men and their helpers were slow—to one afflicted with the American tempo, exasperatingly slow—but thorough. Poco á poco; or, Little by little, is a rule to which labor in Antigua adheres without deviation. And, since the Popenoes themselves, as

already suggested, were in no haste to complete
the job, they let the men go on in their own way,
at their own rate of effort. They were true artisans,
paying no attention to time, often forgetting to
eat, working till darkness surprised them, and taking delight in their toil and its results.

Pop and Dorothy paid them well above the
usual local scale of wages, but even so that did
not amount to very much in American currency.
Arturo, for example, received eighty-five cents a
day, which in Antigua, however, had the purchasing power of four or five dollars in New York
or Boston: for in Antigua one could buy from
twelve to eighteen tortillas for a penny, two or
three large avocados for the same sum, a chicken
for six or seven cents, a turkey, a baby pig, or a
lamb for between a quarter and a half a dollar;
a pineapple for two or three cents, three oranges
or a half-dozen bananas for a penny, and all the
vegetables an average-sized family could consume
a day for two or three cents.

And so, at this rate, by the end of 1932 only the
kitchen and one bedroom, or about one-sixth of

the house, were completely restored; while in parts of the rest of the building tile was being laid on the roof as the Indian tile-makers brought it down from the hills.

However, with most of the débris and dirt removed, the essential quality of the whole restoration, as Dorothy visioned it, was already evident, if not striking; and she had the plans for the rest of the job worked out on paper in every detail.

During this time in Guatemala she bore two children, led an active social life in the city, took trips alone and with Pop and friends, was closely interested in the Servicio Tecnico and Pop's other work, and wrote and illustrated a little history-guidebook of Antigua, entitled *Santiago de los Caballeros de Guatemala.* This she originally intended to issue privately in pamphlet form to be distributed locally as a source of information to tourists who came to Antigua, but the Harvard University Press saw fit to bring it out between covers in 1935.

The death of Dorothy Popenoe

THE DEPRESSION CONTINUED . . . THE BANANA
business in the United States suffered with other
industries . . . and by the middle of 1932 the
United Fruit decided to postpone its development
on the west coast of Guatemala and, together with
the International Railways of Central America,
withdrew the subsidy of the Servicio Tecnico de
Cooperación Agricola.

Wilson Popenoe was asked to reëstablish his research headquarters at Tela, and he did so at once; while Dorothy, resting from her last confinement and taking steps to give up her residence in Guatemala City, stayed on in the high country through the wet season, mostly in Antigua, making an occasional trip to Tela, to see her husband, to engage new household help, and to prepare for the children's return.

She had so worked out her plans for the restoration of the Casa del Capuchino that during the next couple of years Jorge Benitez and the workmen would be able to continue the task without her, but she meant to come to Antigua every few months—it was but a two-day trip from Tela—to see how they were progressing.

From the ship taking her to Honduras on December twenty-third Dorothy wrote to her friend, Thomas Barbour, of Harvard College (who, incidentally, was then writing an introduction to her book) : "We have been transferred back again to Tela and . . . I am now ready again to struggle with the problems of the Ulua Valley pottery." She simultaneously wrote also to a number of other friends, among them Blair Niles, who had lately spent some time with her in Antigua, gathering material for *Maria Paluna*, a novel of sixteenth-century Guatemala. But, although it cannot be doubted that Dorothy did not like this sudden return to the hot and dank Honduran jungles, not the least hint of complaint, regret, or self-pity crept into any of these letters, nor into anything else she wrote or said at the time.

She took things, good and bad, as life offered them to her, and made the most of them.

Dorothy arrived at Tela the day before Christmas. Pop met her at the dock. She looked extremely well and was in her usual high spirits.

"How's the house?" Pop asked her eagerly. During their separation he had been receiving from her long letters about the restoration, in which he was as passionately interested as she.

Dorothy replied it was beautiful and would be more and more so. She had had such fun working on it, and the prospect that it would eventually be their home was almost too good to ever come true.

They spent the holiday together, talking mostly of the house in Antigua. Their friends no longer chided them about it, and Pop and Dorothy thought it would surpass their dream of it two years before; and it would be finished sooner than they had expected. After it was completed—perhaps in 1936 or '37—they would spend all their vacations there and, when they were not there themselves, invite their friends to go to Antigua and stay in the house. Then . . . in 1945 or '50 . . . when Wilson retired on what they were saving from his salary, they would move there permanently. They agreed they would never sell or rent it.

In the morning of December twenty-ninth, Pop was required to fly to Puerto Castilla on Company business. He was to be gone less than a week. On his return he would go back to Antigua with her for a few days. He wanted to see the house.

The next night Dorothy was seized by violent

convulsions, accompanied by nausea. She called the surgeon-physician at the Company hospital. She suffered horribly, but discussed the pains with the doctor as a phenomenon—as something that must be dealt with as intelligently as possible.

Appendicitis? . . . Had these pains some connection with the severe internal injuries she had suffered while engaged in war work seventeen years before? . . . Was this sudden attack aggravated by the fact that for supper last evening she had eaten a little akee? Akee was a curious African fruit domesticated in Jamaica, that Pop was growing experimentally in Lancetilla. If improperly ripened and slightly rotten, it was known to cause intense convulsions and nausea.

The doctor wired Pop for authority to operate.

Emerging from the ether, Dorothy had no severe pains. The operation seemed successful. Then, a few hours later, she suddenly lost consciousness, never regained it, and died a few minutes before Wilson Popenoe reached her bedside.

Pop completes the restoration

Unable BECAUSE OF HIS WORK TO RAISE HIS
children personally, Wilson Popenoe was fortunate in that the widow of a cousin of his, living
near Washington, D. C., who had children of her
own and for whom he had a high regard, offered
to take them into her home.

Pop visited the Casa del Capuchino soon after
Dorothy's death. It was her house. He went over
the plans with Jorge. The restoration should be
completed.

[229]

But not really completed. The northwestern corner of the large quadrangle surrounding the main patio, which was all but hidden by the trees, Dorothy had wanted to leave in ruin. Earthquakes had been part of the career of the house, and she apparently thought that it would be fitting not to wipe the marks of disaster from it entirely. She had planned to let the coffee trees planted in that corner fifteen or twenty years ago remain; and, where no coffee trees grew within the roofless walls, to erect a tiny wooden building which would enclose modern plumbing.

During the four years following Dorothy's death, the work on the house went on slowly. Pop came to Antigua whenever he could for a day or two, sometimes only for a few hours. In 1935 he began to spend his vacations there: a week at Christmastime, a week or two in June or July, when his children came there from the States for their holidays.

As the rooms were restored one after the other, he placed in them the furnishings Dorothy had accumulated and he bought additional pieces in keeping with the others. He acquired old portraits of people who had lived in Santiago de los Caballeros before 1773 and hung them on the walls of the sala and the other rooms. One of these was the already mentioned portrait of Lorenzo Montufar, another of Hermano Pedro de Betancourt, a third of General don Francisco Rodriguez de Rivas.

In Guatemala City he met a young native artist, Humberto Garavito, who had studied in Paris, and he commissioned him to make copies of a number of other portraits, including those of Fray Rodrigo de la Cruz and of Sister Berengaria, the nun who had been the convent cook for twenty-odd years and then become the Abbess of the Santa Clara.

Garavito also painted a portrait of Dorothy from a photograph; it now hangs in Pop's room.

As early as 1933 the Casa del Capuchino—though some of the townspeople were starting to call it the Casa Popenoe—commenced to develop fame as an extraordinary place. Tourists from the United States and Europe wanted to see it. Guides, employed by the various steamship and travel agencies, began to take crowds through it; unfortunately, each contingent seemed to include a few petty vandals . . . and, as suggested in an early chapter of this book, Wilson Popenoe reluctantly instructed Maria to let in, when he was not there, only those who had a card from him.

But even so, in the last three or four years, thousands of persons living in various parts of the world (most of them in the United States) have seen or heard of the house. Nearly every one who visits it is strangely impressed and excited by it.

In conclusion
THE VISIT

I meet the maestro

ODDLY ENOUGH, I CAME TO THE HOUSE ON THE
very day the restoration was, at long last, completed. In fact, I arrived at almost the exact moment that Arturo the mason put the finishing
touch on the fireplace in the library, which was
the last thing done.

Showing me through the place, Pop—as I eventually took to calling Wilson Popenoe—introduced
me to Arturo just as he was gathering up his tools.

[235]

The House in Antigua

A squat, middle-aged man, with a large head and features that were somewhat dull when in repose, Arturo had an attractive smile and an agreeable manner. His mason's apron lay folded on the floor. His thick, hard hand was still powdered with the dust of his last task as I shook it; and he seemed embarrassed for a minute when, using every Spanish adjective denoting excellence I knew, I tried to express my admiration of the house and his work.

"Oh, this is nothing, Señor," he hastened to say, "nothing at all. Come with me, please, if the Señor Doctor will be so good as to excuse us, and I will show you something that is *truly* magnifico."

Pop helped me to understand him; whereupon Arturo conducted me to the part of the house left in ruin, and into the little wooden structure concealed behind a half-ruined wall and the colorful mass of mock-orange shrubbery.

Amused and curious, Pop followed us.

We entered the bathroom; and, his face in a proud glow, Arturo indicated the modern plumbing, especially the part called inodoro (odorless) in Spanish. I was unimpressed. He pointed ecstatically at the chain and the water-box from which it depended. I was puzzled. And Pop, too, did not understand what Arturo was driving at, and he asked, "What do you mean, Maestro?"

Arturo pulled the chain and cried, "See?"

I said I did see, but what . . . ?

"It runs!" he exclaimed. "The water runs!"

To the man who had done most of the actual manual work in restoring the house this modern inodoro, with which he had had nothing to do (it was installed by a Guatemala City plumbing firm), was the most wonderful thing in the place!

Maria serves lunch

AFTER POP HAD TAKEN ME THROUGH THE house and told me a good deal about it, and I had cleaned up a bit, Maria called us to lunch, which she served in the kitchen.

She began to call me "Don Luis," and she laughed as though addressing me thus was a great joke. Her dark eyes glistened with joviality. She knew no English and was distressed that my Spanish was so limited. Nevertheless, we managed to understand one another.

[238]

The Visit

She was exceedingly happy when I asked for a second helping of the thick meat-and-vegetable soup or stew, whatever she called the tasty dish she served us. The rest of the repast consisted of mashed avocados with onions and the merest touch of garlic, which we ate spread on toasted tortillas; and fresh native pineapple (the best I ever tasted) and coffee grown on the premises and cured, roasted, and ground by Maria herself.

Pop was glad I had come, and made no secret of the fact; while, on my side, I felt curiously satisfied that he liked me. I had been in the house only an hour or so, but already it seemed as though, instead of having met him for the first time on that one brief occasion in New York two weeks ago, I had had him for a friend most of my life.

He ate little and talked to me all through the meal, answering my questions about the house, its early history, the restoration, and Antigua. But he was all reticence when asked about himself and his work. What little he told me—then or later—I contrived to draw out of him only with the most direct and persistent queries, and with deliberately erroneous remarks which he could not let go uncorrected.

After lunch, Pop and I sat awhile on the cypress-shaded corridor, talking; and I began to get a feeling that I would write about the house.

Pop and I visit the ruins

THE REST OF THE AFTERNOON POP AND I SPENT wandering through Antigua . . . and I suppose that nowhere in the world to-day is there to be seen another such exhibition of Nature's power to wreck man's strongest works. Pompeii and Herculaneum were buried beneath ashes and lava, but dwellings, temples, and other buildings were not crushed and broken by the quaking, buckling earth as they were in Antigua. . . .

Three blocks from the house was the great ruin

[241]

of San Francisco. Agua, now without the cloud-ring around it, loomed majestically above the shattered masonry, and seemed even bigger than when I had first seen it. The westering sun was now full upon it, and by the woodsmoke rising from the huts I could distinguish tiny Indian settlements on the immense slope which my host pointed out to me.

San Francisco occupies more than a city block; it was one of the most imposing edifices in the old Santiago de los Caballeros de Guatemala. The main church structure is now like a colossal skeleton: the roof is nearly all down, but the windowed walls, though badly fissured, stand . . . and as one looks up, with the sun pouring through the vast holes that once were ceilings, there is something infinitely moving about it.

Pop was amused when I remarked that the place probably looked better in this condition than it had before the earthquake. Elements had touched it intimately, and made it more dramatic. . . .

A group of boys were playing hide-and-seek in San Francisco as we passed through it. The ruin provides an ideal scene for this game. Underneath the wreck of the stately structure of still-standing walls, colonnades and arches, and the fallen fragments of arches, are dark dungeons, chambers, crypts, galleries, and secret passages, in which the boys seemed to move with aplomb and feel entirely at home.

A small part of San Francisco is "restored," but badly. There are a couple of sad altars, a holy-water fount, two rows of pews. A crypt in the wall holds the remains of Hermano Pedro, its biggest asset. Numerous candles burn in front of the crypt all day long, and there is seldom an hour that some one is not kneeling before it.

Not as affecting as San Francisco, but otherwise perhaps even more impressive is La Recolección, on the city's edge, amid coffee fincas, which we crossed or passed getting to it. The coffee trees, being full of red "berries" just then, looked very nice. The people working among them, however, Indians and mestizos, appeared pitifully shabby and starved in body. They received only ten or fifteen cents a day, and their employment was irregular. . . .

La Recolección also sprawls over an entire block. The earthquake lifted the entire front of the church, with its immense columns, statues, stucco work and stone carvings, and hurled it down with such force that, to all seeming, every fragment rebounded and turned round about, so that now great slabs of the façade, lying among the brush and gigantic weeds, actually face what is left of the edifice. Some of the walls of this building, which included an immense cloister, were seven, eight, and even nine feet thick; now their boulder-like fragments fill the vast nave as a handful of pebbles might fill a broken teacup.

In the Capuchin ruin, which takes in a wide area in the center of the city, little is left of the church proper; the extensive cloisters, however, built in two storeys around numerous patios, are in good condition. They are full of unexpected curves, corners and passageways, and are alto-

gether weird and gloomy, although entire wings
are occupied by families and small workshops.

Pop had had the foresight to bring a flashlight
with him; and, crawling in the subterranean passages and dungeons, we came to a large room, very
dank, awesome and dismal, circular in form, and
its ceiling supported in the center by an immense
pillar, shaped like an hourglass. For what purpose
could the holy sisters have used this chamber? To
punish one another, or those who infringed on
the rules of the sisterhood? . . . Later it occurred
to me: perhaps Juana Ocaña, the crackpot woman
during the earthquakes of 1730, had been confined here. . . .

Outside, in one of the courtyards, we came on
niches in the walls where, to test their faith and
stamina, novice nuns were required to stand erect
(so the story goes) for hours at a time while from
little holes pierced in the stone above them drops
of water fell on their heads.

The Cathedral appears fully reconstructed from
the outside, but within it is still mostly a ruin;

only two chapels are more or less restored, and neither too attractively. A priest lives on the premises. There was no one praying inside when Pop and I went through the church.

In one of the restored chapels we paused for a moment before the tomb of Pedro de Alvarado.

But, to me, even more interesting than these—and other—great ruins were the small half-wrecked or partly restored and inhabited houses along the streets where we passed. I could not resist glancing into the patio wherever a door was open. Some of the inner courts seemed to me very attractive; most, however, still contained piles of débris dating from 1773 and before.

Coming from the Cathedral, Pop and I visited the nearby Colonial Museum (formerly the University of San Carlos), which exhibits a few interesting religious paintings, an amusing old wooden statue of Santiago on horseback, and some instruments of torture from the days of the Inquisition.

We went through the restored Hospital of Hermano Pedro de Betancourt, now under the control of the municipality and two or three doctors. It is a small place, inadequately equipped, and none too clean. I was amused by this custom: when a woman with small children enters the hospital, she brings them along and they live with her in the same room, unless, of course, her illness is contagious.

Pop pointed out the sites occupied once upon a time by the birthplace of Rafael Landivar, the poet, and the house in which Bernal Diaz del Castillo, the conquistador-author, spent his last years and wrote his *True History of the Conquest of Mexico*. He showed me also the building, badly ruined, that once housed the second printing press on the American continent; the former Mint; and the Casa los Leones, partly restored, now the local office and warehouse of a Guatemala City sugar firm! . . .

We crossed the Plaza, which is hot and over-bright with sunshine around the park in the afternoon, but always agreeably cool under the pepper-trees. We looked at the incompletely restored Palace of the Captains-General, now housing the

[247]

post-office and the headquarters of the jefe politico, the alcalde, the chief of police, and sundry
other officials. Seen from the park, the Palace
looked in excellent condition; in back, however,
the courtyards (in one of which Don Teófilo de
Alvarenga was hanged) are still scenes of wreckage.

We passed through the Jesuit ruin, but less to
see the masses of broken masonry than the market,
which, it being Monday, was in full swing even
at that late hour; teeming with hundreds of Indians and Indian women of all ages down from
the hills, selling their wares, or else starting to
depart. This was a rich scene, full of color, movement, and smells—none unpleasant.

Here were people not only from Antigua and
immediate vicinage, but from distances as far as
twenty, thirty miles away; from Chimaltenango,
Tecpán, San Lucas, and communities near Lake
Atitlan: mostly Indians, clad in a great variety of
colorful costumes, according to the tribe to which
they belonged.

Especially striking, both in personality and costume, were the Indians who came farthest from Antigua. On their faces were the subtle markings of the centuries and the millenniums, mingled with the brutal scars of the Conquest, not yet erased, as they were for the most part from the faces in Antigua, where the races intermixed, as already told, perhaps more thoroughly than anywhere else in Guatemala.

Most of the articles and produce sold on the marketplace were brought there by cargadores, who carried the burdens strapped on their brows and skulls and partly resting on their backs, as they did in the late 1770's when they moved the capital from Antigua to Guatemala City, and for hundreds and perhaps thousands of years before that.

For this burden-bearing they are trained from early boyhood to youth. Reaching adulthood, they can carry between one and two hundred pounds a distance of one hundred miles in a few days. They half-run most of the time, whether uphill or downgrade. Running is easier for them than walking. And every cargador is said to have

[249]

his favorite weight. If one is used to hundred-pound loads and is hired to carry only ninety pounds, he usually adds ten pounds of rocks or earth to the burden: for one hundred pounds is an easier weight for him than ninety!

The cargador is often a tiny gnome-like man, and earns only a few cents a day—just enough to keep himself in strength, which he does by eating two or three avocados and a dozen or so tortillas a day.

During our wanderings amid the ruins Pop and I met several times a, to me, extremely curious religious procession, which wound through the various streets and bypaths of the city. It began in one of the churches at four o'clock and went on till midnight, ending with entirely different participants than it had begun with.

There was no priest. Four men carried a figure of the Virgin on their shoulders, while around and behind them walked about a hundred persons, mostly women and children; a few of them burning candles, others tinkling little brass bells; some praying, but most of them just walking slowly—

poor and lowly people, humble, smiling to us as Pop and I paused on the sidewalk to watch them.

They walked awhile—for ten, twenty minutes, a half-hour, or an hour, however much time they had; whereupon others stepped in, and the procession continued. The men carrying the Virgin were relieved every now and then, as were the persons with the candles and the bells—not by anybody's order, nor in compliance with some schedule, but voluntarily, or as a matter of custom and duty in the community.

"There's Maria," said Pop as we met the procession the second or third time, at about five-thirty o'clock.

Carrying a candle, which she was trying to keep from going out in the light breeze at the street-crossing, she did not see us. In the procession were also her three daughters: Julia, now eighteen; Victoria, sixteen and a half; and Conchita, twelve.

The sun was setting.

"But don't worry," remarked Pop, "Maria doubtless has the supper cooking or all ready for us. She's a good old soul."

We laughed.

[251]

"There's something about it——"

WE RETURNED TO THE HOUSE IN DUSK, WHICH
lasted only a few minutes; the change from full
day to complete darkness is swift in Central America. But the half-light was long enough for me to
have another look at the house, which, somehow,
now that I had seen the ruins of Antigua, seemed
even lovelier than it had appeared to me earlier
in the day.

My visit to the ruins had somewhat depressed

me. Walking home, I had felt tired. Now, in the house again, weariness seemed to leave me.

Maria and the girls got back from the procession. Julia made a fire in the library. Her mother asked Pop when we wanted supper. There was no hurry. "Muy bien, Señor."

We sat down before the fireplace . . . and, after awhile I remarked to Pop that ever since lunchtime I had been turning over in my mind the idea of writing about the house—perhaps a book.

He seemed embarrassed for a moment and changed his position in the chair, nervously; then, after the slightest hesitation, he said quickly, "All right—all right—go to it."

I said I would need him to help me. He had already told me most of the story in rough outline. I would have to have more details. Had he any written "material," any notes pertaining to the house?

Pop rose, opened an antique cabinet, and presently pulled out a large, bulging envelope.

[253]

The House in Antigua

"This looks like a lot of something or other," he smiled, "but there really isn't very much material here, nor, I'm afraid, anywhere else—just a few old documents—and some notes of facts—data—pertaining to the pre-disaster era of the house and virtually nothing about the first hundred and twenty years of the period during which the place was in ruins. A few of the documents came to us with the deed, and Dorothy saved them. I think she meant to write about the house some day, though that wasn't the only reason for keeping them. They belong here. . . . Then, during the past two years or so, I got from various sources the rest of this, which, as I say, isn't much—but you may be able to work out something from it. I'll be here about a week longer, and we can go over it—you and I—go over it and talk about it."

"Fine," I said, "we can go over it," echoing his suggestion, "and talk about it; then I may be able to reconstruct the story. I don't know, but a few facts may be all I'll need; and it won't be serious even if some of the facts are not one-hundred-percent sure and verifiable from every angle. I mean that it's not terribly important just how long Don So-and-so lived here during the middle of the seventeenth century. Important is the truth-as-a-whole about the house. There's something about it —— "

I paused, uncertain.

"What?" smiled Pop, looking at me.

"I don't know," I said. "I'm just wondering."

"A few others who have been here the past few years," said Pop, "have made remarks to that effect. They couldn't explain what they meant."

"Perhaps I can't explain, either," I said. "I'm just thinking aloud, or trying to . . . but I guess the 'something' that some people see or sense when they visit the house is the rather apparent beauty of the patios and the building, of the whole set-up. There is great simplicity here; austerity. There are good proportions, form, color; also a deep romantic, dramatic quality, which pulls at something or other in all of us that is very vital. I think this was true of the people in New York who first told me of the house, before I met you. . . .

"Then, too, some of us who visit the house feel the breath of antiquity. We are drawn into the past. We sense the centuries, and are awed and often smitten with inarticulateness. The part of the house left in ruin contributes to this sense. All kinds of things have happened here. It's an old house. Three hundred years: that's something to us on this continent. Almost unconsciously we wonder: who has lived here? What sort of people? What has happened to them?

"We—some of us—ask this in connection with almost any old house. Here, in addition, the house was violently, dramatically destroyed in 1773 with the rest of the city by forces beyond human control; it lay a wreck for over a century and a half; then you and Dorothy came along and restored it, which essentially is even more dramatic than the destruction—something intensely wonderful.

"Here is the whole struggle of Man versus Nature. Here is man at his best: the builder, creator: the rebuilder, re-creator, struggling not against himself man, but against a greater, more powerful adversary. Here Nature challenged him, tore

[256]

down his handiwork; he accepted the challenge and the house is up again, perhaps better than ever, challenging the elements. That's something!

"Here we are face-to-face with that great, most dramatic riddle, Time, in which Man is deeply and helplessly involved. . . ."

Later, not in conversation with Pop, I tried to elaborate this explanation of the "something" felt by people when they visited the house.

The house was in Antigua: and Antigua, it occurred to me—this pile of great ruins and half-restored dwellings, inhabited by these pleasant, graceful people; with these extinct and active volcanoes surrounding it and the possibility of more earthquakes, and this house, which was like a flash of near-perfection in a maze of wreckage—was rather symbolic of the world, which, by and large, contained and included fine things, wonderful people, good tendencies, and great promises and potentialities, but was (and always had been, more or less, both essentially and in endless particulars) really a Ruin, a Mess, a Wreck. And just

[257]

now—what with Spain and General Franco, Hitler and Mussolini, the Moscow Trials, the danger of a new world war; the floods, dust-storms, soil erosion, and the impending socio-political struggles in the United States, to mention nothing else —it was in very serious danger of becoming even worse than it was, or ever had been.

Those who came to Antigua felt this. I felt it. The ruins were exciting, fascinating, but also depressing. Then, of a sudden, amid ruination, this house . . . this very eloquent statement as to what is to be done with ruins . . . this indirect suggestion as to what could be done with the Ruin.

My host is disturbed

POP AND I SPENT THE NEXT FEW DAYS GOING OVER
the "material" pertaining to the house and discussing the various details of the story. I asked
him innumerable questions and made notes. Occasionally Jorge Benitez—still a young man, slight of
build, dark, quiet, unassuming—joined us. I talked
with some of the visitors to the house who were
Pop's friends and had known Dorothy. I read or
glanced through the books in the library which

[259]

Pop and I thought might help me to realize the story.

Then I wrote Part One (much as it appears here) and asked Pop to read it. He took it to his room and after awhile came out, worried-looking. He thought it might be all right as a whole, but did not think much of my references to him. In fact, if I would not mind his saying so, he did not like them at all.

The man seemed too good to be true in this day and age, yet here he was—very serious, genuinely embarrassed, almost miserable, on account of what I wrote of him.

I tried to look amused, which I was in part, and said, "But why? What's the matter with my references to you?"

Quite inarticulate for a minute, Pop was nervous, and he almost stammered as he tried to explain that he hoped—that he wished very much I would not write of him so favorably.

I asked him to particularize his objections, and he declared flatly that nearly everything I said about him, as well as the general impression I gave of him, was, to put it mildly, not to his liking. "I know you mean well, Don Luis," as he had begun to call me, "and I'm glad that you think well of me, but why is it necessary to say all that?"

"What would you like me to say?"

"Nothing—nothing at all," he said quickly. "Why drag me in? Why drag in any of that? 'Internationally famous botanist'—my Peruvian doctor's degree—and the rest. Why can't you write your book some way that—" He paused.

"What way?"

"With only Dorothy in the forefront of the story. She's the important figure in it. If you can't leave me out altogether, mention me only as her husband, that's all."

"I never met Dorothy," I said, "while I did meet you in New York and people did talk to me about you, and I did form an opinion of you since I came here."

"But that's all irrelevant. Who cares how and where we met. What's that got to do with the house?"

"I need to explain how I got here," I said. "That's how I write."

"But," he went on, "I thought you would write a book about the house ——"

"That's right."

"—*just* about the house—the restoration ——"

"Yes, but can't you see, Pop: you're part of the story. You belong to the house, or the house to you. . . . But tell me: what's really bothering you?"

"You exaggerate. 'Internationally famous'—that's putting it too strong."

"Your objection is based, I suppose, on the fact that you're not well known, say, in China, nor in Siam, Latvia, and Bulgaria. 'International' means in two or more countries, and Jorge told me you're well known in at least a dozen different Latin-American countries—to say nothing of the United States. So 'internationally famous' is no exaggeration. . . . What else bothers your modest soul?"

He laughed; then, seriously: "Well, I just don't

like it. People will think I got you to come here to
write the book and build me up into a great guy."

"Who'll think that?"

"I don't know; people are liable to think anything."

"What do you care what they think?"

"Now, caramba," he laughed, "you be a sport,
Don Luis . . . you be a sport and fix that up,
somehow. Stick to your title: *The House in Antigua,* isn't it? You write just about the house:
history, architecture, restoration. I asked you to
come here and keep me company; I asked you on
a hunch, for the hell of it, thinking you were a
good fellow; you can't do this to me."

By now we were both "kidding."

I said, "It's about time you learned, Don Wilson, that writers are almost invariably snakes-in-
the-grass. Let this be a lesson to you. During my
cross-examination of you, which, I think, is practically completed, you admitted that you *did* have
a hand in the restoration. You can't deny that.
You came to Antigua before Dorothy; it was you
who found the ruin; you brought Dorothy here;

[263]

you worked with her on some of the plans; et
cetera, et cetera.

"In fact, before you realized with whom you
were dealing, I led you into admitting all sorts of
other things. Also, you blundered in giving me the
liberty of your library, and I have read several of
your pamphlets and magazine articles, which you
are hiding in that cabinet there, and in which you
unwittingly reveal yourself as a very 'great guy,'
a man of importance, and that is what I'll try to
make of you in my book.

"It's about time you got over your modesty. But
I'll be a sport. I'll tone down your history as an
explorer for plants. I'll try to make you write a
book of your own about that some day. I'll mention Lancetilla, but tell very little about the rest
of your work with the United Fruit. And I'll try
to ring in somewhere that you're also a horsethief,
or something like that. . . ."

But, although we finished in joking, Pop was
really uneasy about it all. He wanted me to write
only, or chiefly, about Dorothy . . . and about
Jorge and Arturo. He was very anxious that I un-

derstood just how important Jorge and Arturo had been in the restoration, and he had no reticence in speaking of Dorothy in the most glowing terms.

(I sent him a copy of the first draft of this book, except these final chapters, which had not been completed, with the request for correction of errors in fact. He returned it to me with several corrections and numerous remarks—"Please cut this" or "Who told you this? Please omit"—alongside passages where I mention him and his work.)

Pop is almost wholly uncognizant of his own importance in Central America and in the world of botany and pomology, or he refuses ever to think about it, and is uncomfortable when reminded of it. But in this he is probably not unique among technical and scientific employees of great corporations. I imagine that every great business organization, such as the United Fruit Company, includes some expert receiving a salary not nearly commensurate with his world-worth, who is not generally known outside his field, but who really is a key-man in its day-to-day productive function, and who in his matter-of-fact way performs work that—often unknown to himself—is blazing trails for future technological and scientific progress.

Off and on, Pop and I talked of events in the United States and Europe. He told me he read newspapers and news-magazines very irregularly, and only occasionally listened to radio news broadcasts while travelling on ships; yet he struck me as being very well informed. He is not an intellectual, does not ponder things, but, intuitively intelligent, "goes on hunches."

His biggest "hunch" seemed to be that our so-called civilization—especially in Europe—was in a bad way, and there probably was not much any individual could do right away to make it better, or to keep it from getting worse in the near future. This was more or less in line with my own notions in connection with Antigua as a symbol of the world. He had not heard of Spengler or of Robinson Jeffers before I mentioned them to him, nor of any of the other prophets of disaster; but he believed a new world war was probable before many years passed; and such a conflict, together with the struggle between economic classes, could lead in the long run, he said, only—or mostly—to all-around destruction, a worse mess than we were in now.

He did not know about Europe; but as far as the United States was concerned, he was opposed to both fascism and communism, and was for democracy; however, he doubted democracy could develop sufficient character soon enough to keep going as a general method of dealing with human problems as they arose in the world and in the separate countries, including America.

"But I may be all wrong—all wrong," he added. "Things may not be quite as bad as they appear to be once in awhile. They may be righting themselves without our knowing."

He appeared to me essentially a conservative, in the best sense of the word: wanting to save what good there is in the world, even at the risk of allowing some of the evils to continue for the time being. He has definite liberal tendencies and, American-like, is emotionally addicted to change and progress, but he wants gradual, organic progress, which does not knock down everything on its path; and his mind does not shy of any fact, theory, truth, or viewpoint that is presented to him, and, indeed, he seeks to go to the root of things that interest him.

Dorothy

I DISCUSSED DOROTHY AND THE RESTORATION
with several of the visitors to the house who had
known her . . . and on my fourth day there,
after I had read all her published writings, Wilson
Popenoe handed me another large envelope, with
the remark: "Some papers of Dorothy's," and he
suggested I look them over.

Among other things, the envelope contained
her diary, from which I have quoted at some

length. But I glanced first through her other note-books and was newly amazed by the diversity and palpable systemization and consistent thorough-ness of her interests, which, besides those already indicated, included also literature, art, linguistics, education, culture generally, the problems of women as women, and child psychology. I went over her notes pertaining to the ruin of the Casa del Capuchino and her plans for its restoration.

Then I read the diary, which gradually im-pressed me as extremely illuminating and provoca-tive if taken together with other material and information I had about her.

On my first day in Antigua, after my tour of the ruins, as already told, I had noticed that almost as soon as I entered the house weariness left me and I felt quietly exhilarated. I experienced this a few times later that week, after long tramps through and about the town. Why was that? I did not know. Perhaps the beauty of the house. And the beauty of the house was linked to Dorothy. Some-how, she seemed to live in this patio and all through the place.

The Visit

There had been in her a high vitality and integrity of being that went on after her death; that touched me as I momentarily lived in the house, and urged me to know her and understand the motive power behind the drive of her life.

A friend of hers, who had come to the house to visit Pop one day, had described Dorothy to me as "creative" . . . but I believe that a more accurate word for her was "constructive."

One of the central urges or instincts of her being, as already suggested, was for order. She was for setting right, for repairing, whatever was askew or damaged. Her archæological notebook, like her diary, contains numerous observations hinting that she found endless satisfaction in cleaning and mending the broken artifacts she had dug up. Her first reaction to most things she encountered seemed to have been: what is it?—what is the matter with it?—what can I do with it?

She was always cautious and reflective, whether in her relationships with people or while excavating burials. Possessing all but effortless self-control

and discernment, she could leave a thing or problem alone (as in the case of her little daughter)
and let it take care of itself. It was for her almost
a matter of course to use in the restoration the
able, hitherto unfunctioning people she found living in the ruined house—and, using them, enhance their skill in their trades. She unquestionably touched something in the stolid Arturo that
made him do work such as he had not done before.

Dorothy could be firm and decisive, but was no
fanatic on any subject, as Wilson Popenoe, who is
clearly creative, has been all his life on the subject
of fruit-growing. She was concentrated common
sense, always practical, always direct; and she
could undertake almost anything and do it well;
go into almost any situation and, in all probability, improve it. But she was no mere, ordinary,
plodding, matter-of-fact pragmatist. There was
about her something that inclined a few of those
who knew her best to think of her as bordering almost on the miraculous. I am told that off and on
merely her presence, or but a word from her, was

enough to resolve some momentary predicament in the lives of her friends, to whom she was always devoted and available.

Dorothy was wholly free of fear. "She never hesitated," says Thomas Barbour in his introduction to her little book, "to camp alone at this wild and lonely spot"—the jungle at La Playa de los Muertos on the Ulua River—"among the most notoriously unreliable people in Central America." She made no secret of anything in her life, and had no fear that people might learn something about her and discuss it.

She watched her weight, but merely as a precaution in the matter of health; she was not in panic every time she stepped on the scales, as are so many women. She looked as young and as well as she was; middle or old age had no terror for her; in fact, she never thought of it.

She had no fear of life; *ergo,* none of death.

Dorothy's general effectiveness was due, in great part, to the fact that fear did not crawl through

[273]

her mind and emotions like a slinking cat through a cellar or an attic. Her freedom from fear was largely responsible for the ease with which she learned things, and for her feeling immediately at home in whatever field she touched. The awful mess of the Casa del Capuchino when she and Pop bought the ruin did not frighten her, but released in her positive, constructive energy.

And fearless, she never employed fear to dominate or influence others, or achieve any of her ends. She was for letting people be what and where they were. There was in her no trace of Alvarado. Wherever she appeared, she created a positive atmosphere of good feeling and democratic coöperation.

She had no fear of the future, personal or the world's, immediate or distant, which is one factor in paralyzing or limiting in function most people nowadays, and through them retarding progress everywhere and giving rise to negative national and world movements, both right and left, whose mainstay is terror, more and more fear, which

[274]

can—I am convinced of this—lead only to more ruination.

Among the persons who knew her, more than one spoke of her almost solely in superlatives.

But I think Dorothy knew or felt—if not in her mind, then in her being as a whole—that her worth was for the most part only a potentiality; and, at the same time that she was completely humble and unassuming, she was bent with everything in her to progress toward as full a realization of herself as possible. She was continually implicated in the struggle between her urge toward that self-realization in human fullness and her immediate and very real limitations: and it is not at all extraordinary that some of her friends mistook the intensity of this struggle and her tactics therein —her various tendencies, interests, and enterprises —for greatness itself.

She was not unaware of her shortcomings, although some of them no doubt were ill defined in her mind; and striving for order—chiefly for physical order about her, the orderliness of the effec-

tive executive or the good housewife—constituted
her main or (to us, now) most obvious strategy
in the effort to overcome them, albeit I think that
she was not consciously aware of this, either. The
circumstances of her life in the tropics operated
against her doing sustained work, but she never
blamed them—or anything else, or anyone—for the
interruptions and frustrations she suffered. The
onus was hers; hers the duty to overcome or
change the circumstances, and not the business of
the circumstances to help her.

Dorothy's passion for order could not have been
articulated or realized otherwise than in terms of
physical environment or concrete accomplish-
ment. She was no æsthete dealing chimerically
and superficially with problems of form, tone, or
color. She was living a practical day-to-day life;
whatever thoughts or urges she had were
promptly, automatically, brought to bear directly
upon her activities. Her thoughts and impulses
were no careless, coreless luxuries to dally with.
She utilized them, made them a part of her and
her daily living. And she could make them that

only by performing externally, outside of herself, on the artifacts, on the ruin.

In this Dorothy was typical, or representative, of the best among the competent individualist element of humanity. But then, too, this caused her the occasional feelings of unhappiness recorded in her diary. In the midst of physical order, which she more or less succeeded in creating for herself, she sometimes felt deeply confused.

The explanation for this is that mere physical order, the rigid order of an executive's office or that of a well-organized house, when finally attained, can be—in fact, nearly always is—sterile. It results only in comfort and efficiency, and breeds mostly habit; and this is frequently worse than chaos, from which life is apt to leap at any moment, and often does. . . .

Dorothy Popenoe was intensely alive and as such instinctively opposed to sterility, to mere comfort, efficiency, and habit; but finding herself in this confusion-within-order she scarcely knew what to do about her predicament, which she ill understood. "Feeling depressed again. Seems so silly when I have all in the world I could wish for."

Her formal education in England, as it would have in the United States or almost anywhere else, had stressed facts: what was or had been, not what could be. Education, as we have it, generally does that, and often kills what imagination a person inherently possesses. It had not killed Dorothy's; hers had evidently been too strong for that; but it probably did cripple it a bit, or weighed it down, for a time at least, with huge slabs of data, under which it could not develop naturally. It was just beginning to develop in the years immediately prior to her death.

But Dorothy always knew or felt that there was, or should be, more to human life than mere living and keeping busy in a well-managed house. She needed beauty, that is, *dynamic* (as opposed to mere physical) order. But that need was occasionally painful because inarticulate, unformed, ill satisfied. She wanted to become creative, a maker of that which was good and which would enhance life.

The Visit

This, I think, was the drive behind her trying so hard to function in so many directions, and one reason why her admiration of Pop was so great. In his field, as already suggested, he was really creative. He had done so much for the avocado and banana industries, he had touched vitally so many lives; and here at Lancetilla were these gardens of his, designed to benefit man centuries hence. . . .

This passionate need for beauty and creative function, these occasional feelings of discomfort and confusion within the frame of her well-ordered living, all as yet not very clear in her own mind, were also instrumental in prompting Dorothy into archæology, which is a chaotic, endless mass of puzzles, at the same time that it is an orderly effort to solve them and straighten out the ruins of the past in order to explain the present (that is, face the sphinx Time), and therefore pregnant with life and filled with glorious drama and unending excitement.

Also, archæology yielded beauty and it offered her opportunities to be re-creative, restorative, constructive; to be a discoverer, a scientist—which was the next best thing to being creative, an artist. And it often did bring her extremely close to being creative. It fired her imagination. It logically led her into the task of restoring the Casa del Capuchino, in which she came to the verge of stepping over the line from re-creation to creation, and which, for these reasons, gave her immense satisfaction.

She had never been so happy as she was in the period just before she died, when beauty began to emerge out of the débris and chaos of her ruin in Antigua. With and through the restoration she touched the tangible reality of that which she was instinctively groping for. It gave her a new illumination and power. It was beginning to open the hidden springs of her imagination. It would surely have—had she lived—led to new endeavors.

Dorothy was the clearest case that has yet come to my attention of a person sensitively (even if, for the most part, not consciously) attuned to the promise of human life who tried as hard as she possibly could, and not without success, to contribute to its realization through the development of her own potentialities.

[280]

The Visit

But, lest this attempt at an understanding of her inner being obscure the picture of her more obvious self, which I offer earlier in this book, let me repeat that in her day-to-day, or even year-to-year, life she was simplicity itself: one of the best integrated, best balanced, best functioning, most positive and vivid of human beings. The petty personal problems and inner conflicts and contradictions which periodically convulse, upset, and incapacitate nearly all of us, were largely solved in her case, or had never existed. Her own inner problem, which I have tried to state here, and which she was beginning to solve when death overtook her, was personal, of course; but it was not petty, not neurotic—it was the basic human problem of how to be creative, of how to attain beauty, or dynamic order: which made her into a heroic person in the eyes of her friends simply because her urge or effort to solve it was greater than is to be found in most men and women.

Like her other notebooks and papers which I have seen, Dorothy's diary contains few references to the social, economic, or political conditions and forces in the world. She, obviously, had no great, all-inclusive "social vision," no panacea, no utopian plan. She was, perhaps, mainly unaware of the ferment in the intellectual and political worlds in the late 1920's and early 1930's . . . and the probability is that if it came to a great crisis, say, in the United States, of which country she was a citizen, she would have opposed—along with Pop —any movement for quick, sweeping socio-economic-political changes.

She was aware of the Soviet Union, but little more than that. She had heard of Karl Marx, but only heard of him. She was oblivious of radical journals published in New York, and of their exhortatory editors and contributors. The only important newspaper she read regularly was the New York *Times*; no doubt because she liked it. And I suppose that the people who were running the Red "revolution" in America back in 1931 and '32, and blueprinting the future, would not have thought well of her, had they heard of her and her restoration of the Casa del Capuchino. They would have been quick to label her "bourgeois"

and possibly put her with Pop on the list of po-
tential "counter-revolutionaries" who might best
be "liquidated" as soon as the revolution took
place.

Yet I, for one, believe that Dorothy Popenoe
was geared to progress, to the real, organic proc-
esses of mankind, more closely than were the afore-
said "revolutionists" of the period just preceding
her death, with their excited doings and ideas,
many of which—so far as they applied to America,
at any rate—were akin to the idea that the way to
cure dandruff is to do away with blue serge suits.
Personally, I believe that her restoration of the
house in Antigua was—symbolically or sugges-
tively—a very significant thing, especially if we
look at it from a point that includes a conception
of the world as a Ruin; a Ruin which includes
numerous heaps of débris, containing valuable
materials and fragments.

The painstaking care and patience, the good
taste, the budding sense of beauty, the intelligent
conservatism, the passion to be creative; the realism; the liberal wisdom in dealing with, and using,

the people who lived in the ruin at the time of her taking it over; the urge to get to the base of things and to understand them—the whole mood, attitude, and method of action or procedure that Dorothy Popenoe brought to the task might, I think, well be studied as a microcosmic, but nonetheless very real, example for all who aspire to re-create the Ruin.

The second housewarming

THE RESTORATION WAS FINISHED; THE HOUSE probably was lovelier now than it ever had been during the tenancy of Don Luis de las Infantas, or Don Teófilo de Alvarenga, or Don Rodrigo de Arias Maldonado, or the Montufars . . . and on my fifth day there, as we happened to be discussing Don Luis and Doña Feliciana, and trying to imagine their bendición de la casa three hundred years ago, it suddenly occurred to Wilson Popenoe

to give "a little party," as he called it—"a kind of
second housewarming."

This was on Friday. Pop had to leave Antigua
not later than the following Monday evening, to
take a plane for Honduras early on Tuesday; so
there was not much time for arranging for the
party. "We'll do what we can," he said and, deciding on Monday afternoon, sent invitations to
his friends and acquaintances in and around Antigua, and hired a marimba.

Marimba, he explained to me, was a sort of
xylophone which originally came from West
Africa, where it was the favorite instrument of a
tribe called A-Zandehs, but which the Guatemaltecos developed so that to-day it was "quite a
thing" and the natives claimed it with some justice as their own national invention.

All forenoon and most of the afternoon on Monday, Maria and her daughters were happily busy
preparing for the party. They dashed about, smiling, jabbering, laughing involuntarily at every
word Pop happened to address to them, whether

it was funny or not. This was the first party ever given in this house by the Señor Doctor, whom they obviously adored; and hereafter, perhaps, this noble main patio and this beautiful sala would be the scene of appropriate social affairs. There was to be marimba to-day . . . *marimba* . . . *marimba*—I caught the sound of the word in their chatter every once in a while.

At four-thirty, nine young men came, all part Indian, bringing with them the marimba—a huge awkward contraption. They brought also a bass viol, a saxophone, a clarinet, and a drum; for this was to be no mere marimba, but an entire marimba orchestra.

Soon the first of the invited guests arrived . . . and by five-thirty nearly "everybody" in Antigua was here.

To begin at the top, this included the local jefe politico (governor or chief magistrate), Colonel Carlos Cipriani, a Guatemalan-born son of an Italian father and German mother, who looked to be in his late thirties; an engineer educated in the

United States, speaking fluent English, also German and Italian and, of course, Spanish. We had a short conversation. Beneath his charm and affability I sensed a man of definite views and rigid official competence and efficiency. Pop told me he had high regard for him. In the course of the party some one mentioned to me that the people of Antigua, who by-and-large are not rigid or definite about anything, nor very competent or efficient, had fixed on him the humorous nickname of No-me-toques-que-soy-de-piedra, which may be freely translated: Touch-me-not-I'm-of-stone. Pleading duty, he left early.

Among those present were a number of other local government officials and their wives; the director of the National Agricultural School, located in the nearby town of Chimaltenango, who wore a gorgeous blue uniform with the word "DIRECTOR" embroidered on his chest; Señor Pedro Cofiño, the local garage-owner and agent of Fisk Tires; and Señor Jorge Mann, the German hotel proprietor in Antigua, and his wife, who is of German and English extraction but a native of Guatemala City.

The Visit

I talked with the Manns, and, on learning that originally I was from Yugoslavia, Señor Mann told me that during the World War he had lived for a year in Serbia as a soldier in the German Army of Occupation, and that he had become very fond of the Serbian people. . . .

There were Joseph Henry Jackson, book critic of the San Francisco *Chronicle*, and his wife, who had been in Guatemala for two months, gathering material for a travel book, and happened to be in Antigua that afternoon.

Jorge Benitez came with his wife and her two younger sisters, daughters of a local business man; all three very handsome girls—especially, I thought, the youngest, who was probably in her mid-twenties, quite dark and Indian-looking, with a curious nobility in her features.

"Maestro" Arturo, in his Sunday-best, and his wife, a tiny, diffident woman, quite Indian, came and had a drink and a bite of food; but not accustomed to social life, they soon disappeared.

When the sudden darkness fell, Julia and Victoria lit the candles in the sala, the oil lanterns in

the passageways, the many colored Chinese lanterns in the patios, and the logs in the new fireplace: all of which gave the house a pleasantly
weird aspect. But the nearly full moon, that came
up about seven, made the lights almost unnecessary and the entire scene even more weird and
beautiful.

For a time, the talk was mostly about the house,
the restoration. Some one remarked to me that it
was a shame Pop had to leave to-night, after having been here only a little longer than a week; that
it was too bad he could not spend more time in
Antigua. . . .

Some, talking with me, expressed interest in
the seamen's and longshoremen's strike in the
United States, which was affecting business, nota-
bly the tourist trade, in Guatemala. What sort of
man was this California leader of maritime work-
ers, Harry Bridges? Was he a communist? . . .
Did I know John L. Lewis? What was going on in
the States? What about these sitdown strikes, of
which a New York radio commentator had spoken
last night? . . .

The Visit

Had I seen Carlos Chaplin's latest film *Tiempos Modernos*? It had played in Antigua two weeks before. . . .

Meanwhile other guests danced in the sala and on the corridor.

The marimba boys played almost incessantly. Maria took them drinks and food, and the evening was still very young when the marimba-men proper and the drummer began to sing at the same time that they beat on their instruments.

Spanish-American songs have something that puts a hook into one. Especially moving was a Mexican piece called *Cuatro Milpas* (Four Cornfields) which the men sang and played several times—

The four cornfields, so lonely, remind me
Of the ranch I left behind me, Ah!
And this little dwelling, so sadly it's telling
Of joys that were mine.
No more cows running over my ranches,
And no birds are in the branches, Ah!
No doves now are flying,
And ev'rything's dying,

The House in Antigua

No grapes on the vine.
Use your dark eyes for seeing
How things have ceased being,
There's nothing but waste over there,
And this little white dwelling,
So sadly it's telling,
Of joys that were once ev'rywhere.

Through the palm-trees the winds now are sweeping,
The lagoon is dry from weeping, Ah!
And this wire-fencing is also commencing
To crumble away.
No more corn in the four fields I cherished,
And my horses all have perished, Ah!
No poppies, no flowers,
No grass in the bowers,
All's faded and gray.
Use your dark eyes, etc.*

The song contains all the pain and pain-transcending joy and power of the lowly peons in Middle America, and all their land hunger and resistance to oppression.

The entranceway was left open, and gradually all sorts of townsfolk wandered in, attracted by the marimba. The space beneath the Moorish arch

* © By Edward B. Marks Music Corporation.

of the zaguan was crowded by six o'clock; then the people, young and old—*really* "everybody" in Antigua—began to spread into the corridors.

Among them I noticed the woman who had walked past me with the water-jug balanced atop her head while I stood in front of the door waiting for Maria to let me in a week ago.

Everybody behaved with exquisite dignity; there was no noise, no shouting. They listened to the music, some joined in the singing, especially when the song was *Cuatro Milpas*. This gave the party a spontaneity I have seldom witnessed. It was all so natural, so very pleasant.

Delighted, Pop was for feeding the multitude, but Maria said there was not enough food in the house for everybody and she could not get more anywhere that time of the day. She had not expected "the whole town to come in." There was only some cheese and cake, which she cut, and Julia, Victoria, and Conchita passed the slices around as far as they went. Some of the people got nothing, but this did not matter. They had not expected to be fed.

Their bodies swayed with the music.

A little boy, ten or twelve years of age, rather
dark and very finely made, suddenly took to danc-
ing on the patio lawn in the moonlight. His name
was Tito; just an urchin, barefooted, his blue
dungarees almost in rags—but in that light, spin-
ning around himself, smiling faintly with a mystic
inner delight, he was an ariel, a sprite, a tiny satyr
—a wonderful, precious creature.

A natural dancer, Tito immediately drew all
eyes to him.

His dance was somewhat like a hesitation-walk:
a step, the other foot drawn up to it and held;
then a repeat with the other foot leading, and so
on; each beat of music used for a step, draw, and
hold. But while this was always the basic movement, Tito varied the way of executing it. He
stepped right and brushed left, instead of draw-
ing, and the brush lifted him into a hop on the
right; whereupon, landing on that foot, he
stamped and held the other beside it. He danced
within a square; and sometimes at the corners of

the square, or just anywhere, out of sheer gusto, he brushed in and across, hopped, made a light-ning-quick aerial turn, landed and stamped—all on one impulse. Then he stood for an instant, fully poised, his body holding the end of one movement, gathering power for the beginning of the next. His control was complete; his freedom stirring, tantalizing. He was at once the primitive, the child, the artist, an animal.

His head was tilted to one side, the knees bent on the brush and stamp; the small body, strong and crudely perfect, crouched somewhat; the bare toes curled up. His eyes, shadowed by long black lashes, shone moistly in the dim light. He had short thick hair, dark and wild; ears close to the head; small, full lips, parted a bit; and teeth which gleamed white out of the thin nut-brown face.

When the music was tango, Tito held one arm at shoulder level, the other akimbo, as though to take a partner, and his dance changed in mood and style. Instead of brushing, he swept one leg forward to the other in a swift side-arc, inaudibly clicked his bare heels, and held still for an infinity between moments. With each swoop and spin, he seemed to gather himself to his own center, wind himself around the axis of his motion, and stretch tall beyond his height.

The dance, thus executed, had all the quality of a bird's wing dipping or swooping in space as well as a touch of the virile hauteur and sophistication of an adult vaquero snapping a whip or twirling a rope. It synchronized uncannily, not alone with the legato-staccato of the tango rhythm or with its languorous, androgynous sensuality and breath-taking impudence, but with the soft night-cool air, filled with dew and the scent of flowers and green grass.

The boy danced ten or a dozen times before he wearied. Or it may be that he did not weary, but that, an instinctive artist, he quit before his audience wearied or discovered, while he danced, that the night was getting cold.

The people began to leave. By ten o'clock everybody was gone. The second bendición de la

casa had been a success. Pop was glad. It was a
perfect ending for his brief holiday.

Alone again in the house, we talked awhile,
mostly comparing this party with (and speculat-
ing again about) the first housewarming. Three
hundred years, from Don Luis de las Infantas to
the present, had made a difference. Was this progress? . . .

Then I helped to carry Pop's bags to the car
waiting for him outside.

THE END

Acknowledgment

IN CONNECTION WITH THE WRITING AND proofreading of *The House in Antigua* I was aided, in their various ways, by Amos and Louise Buckley, Alex Gumberg and Frances Adams, Sam Zemurray, A. A. Pollansky, Captain George H. Grant of the S.S. *Musa* and others of the United Fruit Company in New York, Honduras, and Guatemala; Dr. Frans Blom and Doris Z. Stone of the Middle-America Research; Blair Niles, Frances

Acknowledgment

R. Morley, Jorge Benitez, Maria Garcia, Gordon Smith and Mrs. Smith; The Rockefeller Foundation; S. S. Alberts and my assistant, Frank Mlakar. My sincere thanks to them. But I owe a special debt of gratitude to Wilson Popenoe.

A number of facts in Part Two are taken from Dorothy Popenoe's *Santiago de los Caballeros de Guatemala.*

The translation of the part of Cortés' letter in the first chapter of Part Two is by J. Bayard Morris.

LOUIS ADAMIC

New York,
June, 1937

A LETTER FROM WILSON POPENOE

Dear Louis:

. . . It was Dorothy's wish that all those persons who are seriously interested in the Colonial period of Guatemala should see the house. Just how to arrange this is a problem which will probably be aggravated after your book is published, for, as you know, I am so rarely there myself to receive the visitors.

Here is a suggestion: If people going to Guatemala will communicate with me I shall be glad to give them a card. When time does not permit this, I think the best way would be for the tourists to get in touch with the agent of the United Fruit Company in Guatemala City. . . .

Ever yours,

WILSON POPENOE

La Lima,
Republic of Honduras,
May 30, 1937

[300]

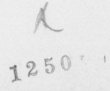